ti

RECORDING THE VISION. MAKING IT PLAIN. THAT YOU MAY RUN.

DEDICATION

First and foremost, I pray that this book brings glory to Jesus Christ. Lord, enable me as I write, and those that read to heed the command of Matthew 6:33:

> "Seek first the kingdom of God and his righteousness and all these things shall be added unto you."

I have chosen to dedicate the writing of this book to a multitude of people because it is through those who have listened to me yap non-stop that I have been able to sift my thoughts in order to write this book. If you have ever been in my presence or talked with me on the phone, this book is dedicated to YOU. Also, those who have encouraged me in any way, as well as my critics and those who speak against me. You have all played an important role in my life and have pushed me to where I am today.

Three special mentions are my Aunt Jo, Aunt Laurie, and Brother Paul Richard Jr. Curran. I can truly say if I didn't have you all in my life, who knows where I would be.

Aunt Jo, you've always told me since I was a child that I could do anything I put my mind to, and I believed you. Life has had its pushes and pulls yet I continually remind myself, "I think, therefore I am". Thank you for the important role you have played in my life!

Aunt Laurie, you have continued to tell me to write a book, and in person it probably seemed like I brushed it off. Your encouragement has had a lot to do with me writing this book, as I remember sitting in the well-furnished basement in Patchogue opening Christmas gifts, and you reminding me that I should write a book. Among many other things, thank you for those nights where you would just sit there and listen to my stories, it really meant a lot.

Poppa Paul, It is truly through you engaging my mind, heart, and Spirit with the Word of God that I am able to be the man I am today. Reading your writings and understanding that I can access the power of God by embracing my vulnerabilities and becoming who I was made, in His image, have allowed for me to grow into a man of God. You have encouraged me with all your being, and helped me dig through the false images and utilize discernment, to recognize my purpose in this world.

Thank You, thank you, thank you.

*Passionately infused with a glimmer of hope
for the spiritually depressed.*

WHAT OTHERS ARE SAYING . . .

Freaked - Out by the New Covenant is an inspiring book, and it's one that drills down into you and resonates emotionally. Its story is not just about another person finding Jesus while behind bars. Instead we find the personal adventure in faith of a young man going far beyond Bible thumping rhetoric. Michael Miano delivers the message of personal growth in Christ and his paradigm shift to fulfilled eschatology in such a way to make for an enjoyable read. Michael's style is unique. He relates his story in easy to read and understandable language, but yet captures a quality and sense in his story, assuring the reader that Michael's journey is unlike what you will find in everyday life.

Miano perfectly captures the essence of spiritual growth that takes hold of him. His story draws us in while watching him wonder about God and the up and down course his life takes after his conversion back in that hard and controlling prison, making it captivating in its authenticity. You can't help but root for Michael to reclaim his first instincts and get back on track. The book will no doubt attract attention for its contemporary focus, and Miano does write movingly, depicting his spiritual journey on that path only few take, but in the end, Michael's struggles aren't unique to any one time or person".

Allyn Morton
Program Administrator of Pastor Training Center
for Fulfilled Covenant Eschatology
ptcfe.com | **preteristvoice**.org

An enthralling tale of passion, grace and fire! That is how I would describe the book you are holding. With every turn of the page you will be climbing the ladder, rung by rung, with a man who refuses to take "No" for an answer. This book is a clinic on how to never give up! Christian Theologian, Clement of Alexandria said, "The seeker shall not rest until he has found . . . To those wise words, Michael Miano is a living monument. Talk about inspiration...this book is an energy drink for the soul!

Frank Speer
co-host The Hairyticks Variety Show
hairyticks.com

FREAKED OUT BY THE NEW COVENANT

By Michael Miano

Foundation

Amsterdam | Singapore | Berlin | Portland

Freaked Out by the New Covenant
Michael Miano

Foundation Press is the non-academic division of Foundation University Press.

Copies of this book may be ordered through booksellers or by contacting:

Foundation Press
Post Office Box 12429
1100 AK Amsterdam, The Netherlands

info@foundationuniversity.com
www.foundationuniversitypress.com

ISBN: 978-94-90179-13-7

design by | **timmyroland.com**

TABLE OF CONTENTS

FOREWORD

Beloved, in the name of our Lord and King, Christ Jesus, may the fullness of Life, Love, and Liberty become your reality.

It is an honor and privilege to write this foreword for *Freaked-Out by the New Covenant*, for many reasons. The first is that I have had the honor, privilege, and frustration (yes, I have gray hair to prove it!) to have my life truly blessed by Michael since 2005. Watching Michael grow in Christ and realizing more of his potential in Christ, has been awesome. As a father, to a son, I am very proud of him for never surrendering, and always striving for the prize. Neither Michael, nor myself, are anything to boast of without Christ. Christ is our provision, strength, and our only claim. Though, knowing the cost to follow and serve Christ as we ought to (especially in the vocation of teacher), it takes a full commitment that many are unable to surrender to. My pride is that Michael is willing to follow Christ, no matter the cost.

The second reason, of many, that I am privileged to write this foreword, is because it brings glory to God through Christ. My being asked to do this is evidence, that despite my "flaws", and the many other things about me that cause people to "scratch their head", asking, "He is a Christian, isn't he?" Christ is still visible in and through me.

As I continue to grow in Christ, I grow in the understanding that when others question our "Christianity", it testifies of His working in, and living in us. The third reason is you. That which Michael and I are called to do is of no use unless others have a thirst and hunger to seek out our King, to add another talent and beauty to the body of Christ. Without you, the body is incomplete, and we are not complete.

I haven't had the opportunity to read the entire "Freaked-Out" book, but through our many conversations, debates, and just our relationship in general, I can tell you that whatever Michael writes herein, is from the heart, and with sincere intent to bring glory to Jesus Christ.

He is truly Freaked-Out, and wholly committed to the kingdom and the kingdoms' advancement. I can also candidly tell you that Michael and I do not always agree doctrinally. This does not mean that we cannot labor in, have fellowship in, and promote the substance of Christ with one voice.

So what does it mean to be Freaked Out? It means to know that all things are possible. It means that we know there is always a way to enter into our promises, if we don't give up on them. It means to boldly speak our convictions, regardless of what others think, feel, or believe. It means we are willing to question "accepted truths", challenge "authority", and never put the manifestation of our salvation in the hands of others.

It means that to obtain an ounce of gold, we might have to mine tons of material that we find no value in, but that which we find no value in is exactly what another has been seeking.

It means we are willing to get out of the boat, in spite of the storms. It means we trust ourselves to His care, provision, and strength to the point that we throw all caution to the wind. Lastly, it means that there is no hope for the world unless we stand to preserve it, and transform it, according to His image, realizing that we, the Church of Christ Jesus, are the only Light, well of Life, beacon of Liberty, and bosom of Love in the world.

If the world decays, darkens, etc . . . our Lord will hold us accountable, because we claim to know.

This is the epistle of God, through Michael Miano, and I am truly blessed to have had the privilege of reading it. And I am confident that I can speak for Michael in saying, we hope to be blessed to read a letter of our Father through you.

To my beloved son, friend, and co-laborer, nothing prevents us if we stick to substance.

Paul Richard Jr. Curran

INTRODUCTION

Deciding to write a book is not an easy task. For a long time now I have been urged to write a book either about my life in the gang world or just my rambling thoughts about being a radical Jesus freak. So, humbly I sit here wondering. Why would I feel inclined to write a book, I'm not important, and even with all the affirmation I receive, I still do not feel as though I have much important information to relay.

Shane Claiborne, a man I have grown to admire by reading and re-reading his books(both *The Irresistible Revolution* and *Jesus for President)* said it best:

> "This book is not an autobiography. I'll leave it to folks like Bill Clinton to write those. I'd feel a bit pretentious writing a book called My Life, and I can't imagine anyone actually buying it, except my mom (who might buy enough to put it on the bestseller lists, but that's not the point). But I do write autobiographically, knowing that a few things have more transformative power than people and stories. People are fascinated by real life and ordinary people, whether it's The Osborne's or American Idol. So that's why I write autobiographically, not because I am somebody so spectacular that everyone needs to hear what I have to say, but just the opposite: I think my experiences have come to exemplify and caricature the struggles and ironies close to many of our hearts".

Thatbeingsaid,Iamgoingtowritethisbookautobiographically. I do feel inspired and burdened to say some things, even if just to share my rants about life. I also feel that if and when I get my thoughts out there (on paper or screaming from a street corner) it will help me clarify the foundational concepts that I stand upon as a **Jesus Freak** living in the New Covenant. It will give me a platform to share these concepts with those who may choose to listen.

All in all, this book is a collection of my rants about life, theology, the Church, and various other things- all an the effort to glorify God and" by some means save a few" (a burden, inspiration and privilege that I will be explain and expound upon throughout this book).

This is not another mere life story of a gang member who has come to the saving knowledge of Jesus Christ, although it would do you great disservice not to acknowledge the saving power of God's grace. Rather, I write to tell you about where I am today and condense the story of how I got here, in all aspects. I intend to answer the question of many who know me from the various walks I've come to in life, "Why is Mike Miano such a Jesus Freak?"

Simply put, I am inspired and burdened by the message of Jesus- the gospel of the Kingdom of God- and feel utterly privileged that I have been led to where I am in being able to share that with you.

Charles Haddon Spurgeon made a great statement in regards to Christians sharing the story of their lives, and I hope that I can write, speak, and act in accordance with his words:

> "Do not go and talk to everybody about what you used to be before conversion as I have known some do. They will almost glory in what they were. I have more than a little hesitation about what is sometimes said

by converted burglars, and men of that sort. I am glad they are converted but I wish there would not talk so much about that which is covered. Let it be covered".

Still, never be backward to glorify God for having covered your sin. Speak of it with delicacy and modesty; but if the grace of God has saved you tell all men of it and do not let people imagine that God has done only a small thing for you. When he saved you it was the grandest thing he could do for you. Do you not think so? Well then, tell the story of it."[1]

Now where do we begin . . . ?

1 - Charles Spurgeon sermon- God's Glory in Hiding Sin

PART ONE

Chapter 1

THE EXODUS FROM GANGBANGER TO INMATE # 04-R-0994

There I was locked in solitary confinement, after a fight turned riot in the prison yard of Coxsackie Correctional Facility. Right then I started to realize- "enough is enough". As I sat there and listened to all the prison gossip-from the latest Jay-Z song, to the fight that had landed me in this dark, quite hole. I was rehearsing my life over and over in my head.

How had I gotten to this point?

Now what?

There has got to be more to this thing called life, right!

Who am I trying to please in life? Is that working,

Who was hurting as a result of my actions?

Moment by moment, I began to contemplate the journey I had been on for the past 2 years. All the prison experiences took their toll and shaped me in many ways, I had excelled in the image of being , a gang leader, studied Islam, considered starting my own religion (probably would have looked a lot like the Gnosticism that plagued the early church), and as

I sat there- I experienced burnout. I've prayed before. In retrospect, God always answered my prayers- the prayers of an ignorant, self-deceiving, selfish young man who cared for nothing but himself. As I sat there, I couldn't do anything but cry . . . and that I did.

There are three genres of text that have always piqued my interest: religious, historical, or controversial. This discovery was made in the 8th grade while making sense of a Christopher Columbus history project - thanks to the teaching efforts of my Aunt Jo, and the wise words spoken by a respected gang leader- concerning studying history to know where you're going. Therefore, it only made sense that while in the New York State Correctional System, S-Block (somewhat solitary unit for the utterly disobedient), I would pick up the Bible, the Qur'an, and various metaphysics books.

At first read, the Bible confused me to the point that I would actually remark to professing Christians that they should "throw the Bible over the prison wall or . . . burn it". The Quran was simple, yet many tenets of Islam didn't sit well with me (ranging from why God hates bacon to the contradicting story of religious history). Metaphysical books such as the Secret Science by John D. Baines, made perfect sense to me but didn't spawn a radical change much other than help me with some morals and give me some "spiritual" self-awareness.

Fast forward four Months to Auburn Correctional Facility which I will forever refer to as the "Iron Furnace". I wanted to go to Protestant Services in order to get me out of my maximum security prison cell for some time. This in turn led to my introduction to a man of God named Paul Richard Jr. Curran at which point my life would never be the same. This is the man that through Godly wisdom and patience led me to Christ Jesus. He catalyzed my journey of missional transformation which is outlined throughout this book. The message of a God who loved me so much that He sent His Son to die for me began to take on a whole new meaning. I had attended Church both in and before I went to prison so "Jesus dying for my sins" wasn't exactly breaking news to me. Brother Paul helped me see the Bible through a socio-political lens, and urged me to find my place in the Missio Dei (Latin: sending of God). All of my concerns, questions, ideas, and backlashes concerning Christianity were met with wisdom under girded by Scriptures from the Word of God. Apathy, seeking approval, even conformity wasn't as acceptable- we were men from God, called by God, led by God, to preach the message of God. All of a sudden, everything just seemed to make sense.

I began reading a unpublished book written by brother Paul Curran called "Walk Toward True Hope and Vision", which detailed the Christian life and explained how the gospel of Jesus Christ calls men to abundant life (John 10:10). Since it was a quest for knowledge that ultimately led me to at least consider what brother Paul had to say about Christianity, I was in awe when I these words that he wrote:

"The treasures that we Christians should be seeking are wisdom, knowledge, and understanding. These are the heavenly treasures which are more precious than gold, silver, and precious stones (see, Proverbs 3:13-15). These heavenly treasures will lead us in the way of righteousness, and they are Jesus Christ Himself"

Therefore, I began to realize that this quest I had been on was somewhat of a journey led by God to draw me back into His embrace. Man, God is good! As we begin to put our foot to the petal so to speak, growing in the grace and knowledge of God, we begin to walk in the true hope and vision for our lives. This is how we make known the manifold wisdom of God (Ephesians 3:10). And so, I continued on seeking, searching, and walking worthy of my calling. The

3

complete destruction of the worldview I once had was pretty simple stuff when I was challenged to see things, specifically in American politics, that I had not seen before. Yet to the discerning eye these things were so clear. A book I had read at that time was Brotherhood of Darkness by Dr. Stanley Monteith. Acquiring all sorts of new insight along with the historical knowledge I had before I even considered the truth of Christianity, it all just began to form a radical worldview. The Biblical message of the kingdom of God being the Truth of all truths, and ultimately the only solution to the ills of the world, this was the message Christ and His followers were willing to die for.

"We do, however, speak a message of wisdom among the mature, but not the wisdom of this age or of the rulers of this age, who are coming to nothing. No, we speak of God's secret wisdom, a wisdom that has been hidden and that God destined for our glory before time began. None of the rulers of this age understood it, for if they had, they would not have crucified the Lord of glory. However, as it is written: "No eye has seen, nor ear has heard, no mind has conceived what God has prepared for those who love him" - but God has revealed it to us by his Spirit. The Spirit searches all things, even the deep things of God.

For who among men knows the thoughts of a man except the man's spirit within him? In the same way no one knows the thoughts of God except the Spirit of God. We have not received the spirit of the world but the Spirit who is from God, that we may understand what god has freely given us. This is what we speak, not in words taught to us by human wisdom but in words taught by the Spirit, expressing spiritual truths in spiritual words.

The man without the Spirit does not accept the things that come from the Spirit of God, for they are foolishness to him, and he cannot understand them, because they are spiritually discerned (1 Corinthians 2:6-14)". Contemplating life, I finally decided to go to Bible study. I still have the notes from that night which turned out to be the first Bible study that ever made sense to me. The study was called the "Iron Furnace". I could never before understand why such a so-called "loving God" had allowed my life to become what it was, obviously placing most of the blame on Him (if He existed).

September 8, 2005

Egypt- "The Iron Furnace"- A Blessing or a Curse? (Acts 7:6) The Lord said that "his" seed, being Abraham's seed, would dwell in a strange land, and would be brought into bondage, and would be treated evil for 400 years (Numbers 20:15). The Hebrews were vexed and worked hard labor in Egypt under the Egyptians for a long time (Exodus 1:13-14).

Why would our merciful God allow the Hebrews to endure this? (Job 23:10), when the Lord tries us, we come forth as gold, just as when gold goes into the furnace and it is shaped, that is what God does with us. The Lord refines us in ways that will lead us to glorifying Him (Zechariah 13:9; Romans 12:2).

Allow the Lord to use you in His "iron furnace", so that you may be made into a beautiful man of God (Daniel 12:10).

After that study, I came to terms with the fact that God had been working in my life for a long time, and that He had me right where He wanted, and I was ready to profess the gospel of Jesus Christ. After sharing my convictions with Brother Paul and being advised to count the cost and consider all the events going on in my life, I was ready! A couple evenings later at the "Christian court" (the tables where the Christians did Bible study) in Auburn Correctional Facility prison yard, I was surrounded by my brothers in Christ and led in prayer with tears and arms held in prayer and solidarity, and committed my life to following Jesus Christ.

"As they were walking along the road, a man said to him, "I will follow you wherever you go". Jesus replied, "Foxes have holes and birds of the air have nests, but the Son of Man has nowhere to lay his head." He said to another man, "Follow me." But the man replied, "Lord, first let me go and bury my father." Jesus said to him, "Let the dead bury their own dead, but you go and proclaim the kingdom of God."

Still another said, "I will follow you Lord; but first let me go back and say good-by to my family." Jesus replied, "No one who puts his hand to the plow and looks back is fit for the kingdom of God (Luke 9:57-62)".

I continued to count the cost of being a devoted follower of Jesus Christ and although I hadn't felt any conviction concerning my membership in the Gangster Disciple Nation, it seemed that some individuals within the Christian community wanted clarification as to where I stood in terms of "choosing one master".

To be honest, I wasn't sure what was going on in my mind and heart, so how could I be expected to offer an explanation? Yet, I felt judged and wanted to do things right, so I continually consulted brother Paul about these things and he would reply that I need to focus on Christ and allow that to simply change me, and he advised me to be inwardly convicted rather than worry about the judgments and notions of others. I wanted to be a leader for Jesus and I dreamed of changing the hearts of many gang members and leading them to faith in Christ, and even to this day have the dream of seeing changed hearts in that lifestyle, but how exactly would that be done? God was still working on me - The Iron Furnace (as He always will be). This change in my heart which in theological terms this would be called regeneration began to have outward expression, and was working on the radical in me. I had always been a radical and not afraid of challenging things, yet little did I know I was about to begin following the ultimate nonconformist- Jesus Christ Himself.

I would soon become a radical follower of Jesus who is zealous for the things of God beyond the bounds of religious conformity. Continuing to read books such as The Satanic Bible by Anton Levy and having conversations with everyone from atheists to the "gods" from the Nation of Gods and Earth, this continued to foster an already engaging, critical attitude toward the "wisdom of the world" that was going on within my mind.

I looked forward to every opportunity in the mess hall or in the prison yard, to somewhat "get on someone's nerves" and preach the Word of God (and getting on people's nerves I did- even to the extent of having the more radical Muslim men threaten me to stay away from conversation with their recent converts).

My radical antics became widespread and earned me titles such as Mikey Bibles and Mikey Scriptures, and even though these nicknames were given in jest, I loved every minute of it. Slowly people started to trust my integrity as a follower of Christ which led to much fruit bearing for the kingdom of God.

Within a matter of months, I experienced my "Timothy moment", when Brother Paul was transferred to another jail (January 26, 2006 to be exact). As he stated and I agreed, it was time for me to leave the nest. Looking back to that point in time, and situations that have occurred since, I realize the real value of our following Jesus comes out when we decide to embrace our calling (leaving the nest, so to speak) and are given the opportunity to grow and show who we are in Christ. It makes sense in the aspect that Jesus Christ did this with His disciples, even to the extent of praying a long, distressing prayer before He was to be taken away from them (John 17 cf. Hebrews 5:11-14).

The mission truly starts when you get out of your comfort zone, and having my mentor leave my side- pretty much the only Christian influence I had at that point- definitely put me outside my comfort zone.

This time helped me to build the foundation of who I was, what I stood for, and what I felt destined to become. I became even more engulfed in sharing my faith. I started writing home to all my friends and family and telling them the amazing realization I had come to in Christ Jesus, and that the Biblical claims of being redeemed by God through Jesus are all true.

I was so inspired by the message of the Bible and wanted everyone to be afforded the same opportunity to know the Truth. I became known as the guy in the prison yard who came out "on mission" to tell someone about Jesus.

I would sit in a fortress of the Scriptures and Christian books - The Cost of Discipleship by Dietrich Bonhoeffer; The Apostolic Ministry by Rick Joyner; The Case for Christ by Lee Strobel; to name a few - during my work hours in the mess hall. When I was back in my cell I was building up my collection of studies by use of a Bible Concordance and the Word of God.

"Praise be to the God and Father of our Lord Jesus Christ, who has blessed us in the heavenly realms with every spiritual blessing in Christ. For he chose us in him before the creation of the world to be holy and blameless in his sight. In love he predestined us to be adopted as his sons through Jesus Christ, in accordance with his pleasure and will- to the praise of his glorious grace, which he has freely given us in the One he loves. In him we have redemption through his blood, the forgiveness of sins, in accordance with the riches of God's grace that he lavished on us with all wisdom and understanding.

And he made known to us the mystery of his will according to his good pleasure, which he purposed in Christ, to be put into effect when the times will have reached there fulfillment- to bring all things in heaven on earth together under one head, even Christ (Ephesians 1:3-10)".

That passage is amazing not only in the context of the Israelite covenant, but also as it so beautifully pertained to my life. As I understood the gospel, sitting in my cell and studying Scripture, I knew that God had called me, formed me, and was continually building me up to be the man He wanted me to be (a process that is still ongoing).

January 11, 2006
Prayer Journal Entry

"The other day brother Paul said something to me that has not left my mind since, "I realize your gift (calling), to show others and to encourage a real relationship with Christ". Also concerning my latest problems of discouragement he mentioned reading John chapter 17 verse 15".

Chapter 2

THE AWAKENING
The Heart of a Christian and the mind of a Berean

"Having then laid aside all false shame, and the inveterate error of mankind, with all its bombastic parade and empty noise, though by means of it you fancy you are possessed of all advantages, do you give yourselves to the things that profit you"

Justin Martyr

As to my desire to learn of Christ, I owe a lot to the reading and studying I did while I was in solitary confinement. I read everything from Mein Kampf by Adolph Hitler, The Prince by Niccolo Machiavelli to John Saul novels. It was little quotes and odd inspirations which have created the thirst for knowledge that exists within me today. Ultimately, it was the thirst for knowledge that urged me to listen to Brother Paul talk, preach, and rant about the things of God. Brother Paul was such an inspiration, because his knowledge and zeal fed my hunger for new revelation and wisdom. His continual urgings for me to find my callings and gifts to serve in the ministry of Christ Jesus pushed me that much further.

I had known that when brother Paul was put on transfer that it would lead to a time of challenge and growth. I began to see the Lord's will moving in my life and submitted to it rather than my own which was quite the humbling experience since I am a pretty darn stubborn person (and still to this day at many times choose to rebel until the Lord seemingly decides to make divine moves). I remember dreaming of crazy adventures and waking up with the last thought being- "Lord, thy will be done". One time, I was given notice that I would be transferred to another part of the jail, the more troublesome side, where my gang tattoos would not be tolerated, and fear crept in. In desperation I prayed and sought a word from the Lord, and the last lines I said were "Your will be done". I had no idea why I was being moved because it made no sense whatsoever. Sure enough, I was moved next to a guy, who was from Long Island (my hometown) who was going through extreme stress and aggravation in life.

One night after all the lights went out, we talked on the gate for hours. Sitting behind the bars of our individual cells which were divided by a concrete wall, I shared the Scriptures with him and we prayed together, and his response was that this night had strengthened his faith in many ways. Oddly enough, the next morning I was moved back to my original location which no explanation as to why I was moved in the first place. Divine coincidence?

Even though I was born again through the Spirit, issues from my past still came up from time to time. An example would be getting into a fist fight with another gang member in the prison yard as I walked back from Bible study one night. I had complications at home with my social life which would get me down at times, but usually I would combat the stress and aggravation by diving into the Scriptures. I was blessed with opportunities to mentor many young men battling with life and faith- some of whom have left my life and influence as quickly as they came and some who I still have friendship with. I became known as the man of God who people could talk to and relate to, as I continually sought out ways to be like the Jesus I read about in the Scriptures, in a modern context, behind a prison wall.

"You will know the chosen ones by the fire that already burns in them. They will never be content with religious practices, for they yearn for me and the reality of this realm"- Rick Joyner, The Sword and the Torch

I quickly became engulfed in the new calling that God had on my life and was searching and searching for His will in my life. What was I to become? I devoured the Word of God in the spirit of the prophecy given to Ezekiel (read Ezekiel chapters 2 and 3). I began to look at life as Christ Jesus walking by my side as a friend, a father, a mentor at all turns- this led me to consult Him at every turn and live a life of radical zeal. Christian rapper Lecrae illustrates this in the song "Don't Waste Your Life" in which he lyrically says in regards to the Apostle Paul, "If Christ ain't resurrected, we wasted our lives. But that implies that all that's built around Jesus being alive". I truly felt and still feel that way about life- it's simply all about Him (Galatians 2:20).

My passion for Christ became evident, even to the extent that it bothered some people- even professing Christians, but it was readily becoming a part of my zealous nature and I just couldn't shake it. I dealt with frustrations from time to time concerning the gang culture- my life, my shame, my calling- as well as frustrations concerning the religiosity of the Christian culture and my calling in that regard. I voiced the words of Isaiah and fully expected for the Lord to "create in me a clean heart", and as a jealous God, He surely did.

"We may become so concerned about what we could be doing for Christ somewhere else that we miss great opportunities right where we are. Paul was writing to say that people should be Christians where they are. You can do God's work and demonstrate your faith anywhere. When you become a Christian you should continue on the work you were doing before, all work can become Christian work, provided it isn't immoral or unethical. Every work can be an opportunity to honor, serve, and speak out for Christ. Because God has placed you where you are, take advantage of every opportunity to serve Him there". (Scripture notes in Life Application Bible concerning I Corinthians chapter 7 verse 20).

My life became a mission of "making the most of every opportunity" to bring more and more people to the realization of Christ Jesus being the incarnation of God for us.

I dreamed of leading GD's to Christ, learned where I needed to draw "lines of distinction" in my life, and was committed to bringing all things to their fullest potential (whether it was living my life as worship to God, the G.D.N. as a positive organization, or leading all people to Christ Jesus). I wanted to fulfill Matthew 28:19-20 by living out I Corinthians 9:22.

> "The Lord has spoken to me through 1 Corinthians chapter 7 verses 17-23, which explains that a Christian is to keep the place in life that they had prior to being a Christian, but now do so for the Lord. This was a clear indictment on my life. I would continue with my involvement in the G.D.N., but now I would serve the Lord and shun evil. We must remember that Christ did not pray to take His people out of the world, but rather to keep them from evil . . .
>
> So now being 'renewed in mind', this has sent me out to accomplish some difficult tasks within the G.D.N. I have sought to be a "light", and use Godly influence in the darkness of "gangs" and violence, and this has not been taken lightly or without opposition from within the gangs and outside them". - Excerpt from a paper I wrote called: *Seeing Men as Trees*

I was eager to be released. That day finally arrived on September 8, 2006. I remember venting to a Christian brother and friend named "Honesty"(who not only shared a cell next to me but also worked with me in the mess hall), and his advice was always appreciated. He was older than I and shared a similar life story, as he was also battling with what really mattered in this life. Many times Honesty would scold me for being a bit too radical (which I always defended and argued with him about), yet he also listened and helped me sort out things going on in my own mind.

Sometimes we just need those people who will listen, let us vent, and in turn we answer our own questions. I was nervous about going home. I didn't know how the transition would affect me, and Honesty would do all he could to give me advice. A point of advice: Take time out to appreciate those people who give you words of wisdom. I have since lost contact with Honesty but I never fail to realize that his listening and bits of advice were so needed at that very moment. Upon release I had many questions: How would I deal with women and live a Christian lifestyle? How would my influence work within the GD's? How much had changed? Worried doesn't seem like the right word, but rather I was STRESSED-OUT!

I knew that upon my arrival home there would be varying expectations as to my "new" character. For example, I knew my family wanted me to pursue a positive route of success and live a good life, the GD's expected me to reform things and put a better organization structure in action, and then the fringe people who knew me expected me to be the same, if not a more hardened streetwise individual than I was before I went to prison. Unfortunately, my people-pleasing attitude coupled with my personal struggles of who I expected myself to be played a role in leading me toward a confused state of mind upon my return "to the world". I had made it clear I was a Christian and wanted to live a life to glorify God, but due to all the expectations and personal confusion, I continually excused poor decisions and tried all I could to sprinkle bits of Bible living into my life. It is safe to say, I wasn't living a life worthy of the gospel or "making the most of every opportunity" as I had previously committed to.

I remember venting to my mother and some friends concerning my failures of living the life that I felt called to live, but no one's advice seemed to offer the encouragement or conviction that I was looking for. I visited some local churches a couple times but they weren't churches where I felt I was being led by or convicted by Scripture, so I lacked the accountability offered by a Christian community.

I have learned through experience that God does His work in us similar to the switch of seasons. Within months, the conviction that I was living a double life had become enough. I remember crying out to God and asking something to occur that would offer stability, accountability, and structure. Around this time, I met a young woman who I was interested in (whether it was a divine God moment or simply a guy meeting a girl, which can and will continue to be a question until the time if and when I can ask the Father, Himself). This relationship provided me with the things I had been asking God for and allowed me things necessary to grow.

As I sit and write this book, I am still dealing with the gains and pains that came from that relationship and season of my life.
The time had come. Confirmation began in my mind, heart, and soul that it was time to begin living the life I knew I was called to live, ultimately bringing glory to God.

Stability is a very important aspect of a focused life. In retrospect I value the stability offered through that past relationship, and learning the lessons from that time. I continually look for areas where I can usher more stability into my life. Although, this much needed and valued stability would in a later season lead to me literally putting my life in the hands of God to be molded and shaped- even at the expense of normalcy.

"In the Gospels the very first step a man must take
is an act which radically affects his whole existence"-

Dietrich Bonhoeffer
The Cost of Discipleship

I continued contact with Brother Paul, which helped a lot because not only was it hard to find a church that offered acceptance and accountability, but truthfully it was just really hard for me to feel inspired to regularly attend any church on Long Island. Brother Paul had dreams and aspirations concerning the end times and wanted to further my understanding about where we were in the prophetic timetable, the times we had yet to face, and my role as a teacher / watchman through all of this.

Brother Paul had a vision he felt was given to Him by the Lord, and many times remarked that I was called to be his "Caleb" in ministry (Caleb being the young man who was willing to go with Joshua into the promised land).

This was applied to the promise that brother Paul felt led to, through the Tribe of Dan Church in Christ Jesus (which would eventually become The Tribe of Dan Ministry).I was willing and ready, therefore we launched the idea, right there in my mother's garage. All the while we had much larger aspirations in our hearts and minds.

Chapter 3

END-TIMER
THE MINISTRY OF A DANITE

"Dan will provide justice for his people as one of the tribes of Israel. Dan will be a serpent by the roadside, a viper along the path that bites the horse's heels so that the rider tumbles backward. I look for your deliverance, O Lord (Genesis 49:16-18)".

"Building an Ark in Truth and Love. Networking for the Wealth of Many" Tribe of Dan Ministry Slogan

Brother Paul Richard Jr. Curran had been blessed with a vision for ministry, yet even to this day, the walls of a New York state prison seemingly hinder him from bringing his ministry vision to fruition. In 2007, I began efforts to work with and assist him in serving Christ through the Tribe of Dan. Being called as a Danite had some implications, necessities, blessings, and requirements- all of which we understood to be expressed through the Tribe of Dan Church in Christ Jesus.

The philosophy and vision of being a member of the Tribe of Dan (A Danite) is based upon the vision given to Paul Richard Jr. Curran, which has basis in the Scriptures, various political views, certain end times views (namely post-tribulation rapture theory), and a practical application of the kingdom of God. The Tribe of Dan is an end-times equipping ministry working toward helping individuals find their callings and life in Christ, all in an effort to better work as "the Church", equipped to face the times of trial in the near future. The Tribe of Dan concept essentially looked to be watchmen/watchwomen who were aware of the coming trials and making others aware.

The Tribe of Dan Ministry sought to be the ark of help when crisis hit whether it was through supplying food and shelter or spiritual support in how to keep the faith and understand how God is working in and through things.

In retrospect, it is easy to see how and why I was involved in the Tribe of Dan, although I no longer share the eschatological (things of the end times) view as this ministry. Nonetheless, the writings and teachings of Brother Paul Curran and my involvement in his ministry has shaped who I am today. One of the first requisites of being a Danite was to be a diligent student of the Word of God, and also to be critical of all things. The practical aspect of being the body of Christ, in Spirit and Truth, was and still is the simple most fundamental aspect of the kingdom of God.

Yet today it is one of the most misunderstood and misapplied concepts in the world, and sadly in the Church too. Understanding my service to God as finding my specific purpose in Him, and how I could serve Him and others best, has been the most fulfilling journey of my life (much of the reason why I write this book).

Around March 2007, I started holding small Bible classes in my mother's garage on Long Island. Usually it was me preaching and teaching my studies and Paul's writings to about 3 or 4 friends and acquaintances every Monday night. That time was such an encouragement to me, yet I remember always feeling bothered and burdened that the message wasn't quite sinking into people's minds the way

I felt it should. Once they left my company did they want to learn more about this Jesus thing? Was anything changing? What was I doing wrong?

"If we try to make ourselves strong, we are relying on ourselves, not Christ. When we allow others, or ourselves to dictate what is good or bad for us, we conform to man's image, not God's image for us. We all have desires, passions, fantasies, hopes, dreams, etc... For these things not to be fulfilled in us, because we choose to repress or ignore them, it is rebellion against God. This is why many Christians suffer frustration because they are working against the will of God for their lives. To the spiritually minded, all things are possible, we will find, we will receive, and the door will be opened unto us. Therefore, those who are living in the Spirit are free, and they live in constant expectation of God fulfilling their desires, and adding to their lives those things which will bring contentment, peace, and joy. Also, every experience is seen as an opportunity"(Excerpt from Embracing Your Vulnerabilities: Accessing the Power of God article written by Paul Richard Jr. Curran).

Unfortunately my life still wasn't being lived to the fullest potential, or in any way to bring glory to God. I had my "faith battles" and usually chose compromise over a full-fledged walking on water type of faith and obedience. I used my criticisms of so-called Christians and the weak religious natured American Christianity to make excuses for myself not living a passionate life for Christ or studying the Scriptures. I felt the urge deep down inside to become whole-heartedly abandoned to the things of God but I allowed my fears, surroundings, and excuses to keep me back. I continually rebelled against what brother Paul was trying to tell me concerning the confirmation of who I was in Christ Jesus. I was clearly battling with a double life which kept me from experiencing the blessings and confidence of walking as a redeemed child of God. Whew, what an experience it is to be fully redeemed, which is something I now walk in regularly, although I have my moments (since as sinners we will always battle with sin).

"At that time the disciples came to Jesus and asked, "Who is greatest in the kingdom of heaven?" He called a little child and had him stand among them. And he said: "I tell you the truth, unless you change and become like little children, you will never enter the kingdom of heaven. Therefore, whoever humbles himself like this child is the greatest in the kingdom of heaven. And whoever welcomes a little child like this in my name welcomes me. But if anyone causes one of these little ones who believe in me to sin, it would be better for him to have a large millstone hung around his neck and to be drowned in the depths of the sea.

Woe to the world because of the things that cause people to sin! Such things must come, but woe to the man through whom they come! If your hand or your foot causes you to sin, cut it off and throw it away. It is better for you to enter life maimed or crippled than to have two hands or two feet and be thrown into eternal fire. And if your eye causes you to sin, gouge it out and throw it away. It is better for you to enter life with one eye than to have two eyes and be thrown into the fire of hell (Matthew 18:1-9)".

Over time, we started different efforts such as working toward publishing brother Paul's books (which I had the joy of typing for hours on end. I mean that both sarcastically and seriously). Brother Paul always envisioned the ministry having its base in the upstate region of New York, something I always debated and argued because I didn't feel the inspiration to go. Eventually, I did listen and went to visit Paul's friends and family, as well as some ministry connections.

The time spent there led to various conversations and debates over views of the Tribe of Dan Ministry, which confused me but also gave me the insight needed to study more and be encouraged by the things of God. Although I felt stuck and hard pressed concerning ministry success.

I knew it was time to move somewhere. I questioned and questioned the Lord on location and purpose all the while trying to avoid the various offers and places everyone else felt I should entertain. I continued in prayer and study, specifically to find who I was and where spiritually I felt called in life- and would allow for that alone to provide some confirmation as to residence location. I knew I wanted to experience refreshment and a sense of church that was a bit less traditional and "dead" as I had seen on Long Island- I questioned, "Is there even such things as a church like that?". Within time, the young woman I was dating and I decided that we would move to Fort Myers, Florida (with the cheapest apartments on Craigslist), and it was then that I stumbled upon the website of Next Level Church.

> "The focus of Next Level continues to be on creating an environment where people of all ages can experience God, worship Him freely, participate in ministry, and connect with others!" - Excerpt from Next Level Church website

There is a lot that entails what occurred as I moved to Fort Myers, Florida, but to make it brief, I fully expected radical life change, and God provided. Jehovah Jireh! Almost immediately, I felt set free and renewed to become the man of God I felt called to be.

The personal plan I had was to immerse myself in the Christian culture that seemed so alive in the south, as opposed to prison and Long Island.

I propelled myself into various ministries and study groups as well as discovered a wide array of Christian books would seemingly cater to the personality I felt welling up inside of my soul. Who knew Christianity could seem so cool?

As the acting pastor of the Tribe of Dan Ministry, I initiated meetings with various local pastors and Christians. I created Myspaces, webpages, and invites for Tribe of Dan activities as well as typing up books and dreaming of my future in ministry. I realize now this is where the radical nature that is alive in me now as far as "evangelism" started because I was in a new place, I didn't know anyone- how would I spread the Word? God readily provided me with an open opportunity to let go of comfort ability and to stretch my personality a bit. Thought after thought, practicality after practicality of envisioning my life in ministry, serving in and through the Tribe of Dan Ministry was seemingly becoming harder to pin point and understand. Understandably, I had put a lot of effort into the Tribe of Dan Ministry, and loved my spiritual father in the faith, Paul Richard Jr. Curran very much and wanted to be a co-laborer with him, yet I couldn't shake the critical spiritual discomfort I was feeling.

Finally, I resolved. I must understand where God is leading me, and follow!

Chapter 4

THE FREAKING OUT OF A JESUS FREAK

"Be devoted to one another in brotherly love. Honor
one another above yourselves. Never be lacking in
zeal, but keep your spiritual fervor, serving the Lord."
(Romans 12:10-11).

John Bradford stood boldly before the Lord Chancellor, "I urge
you", the young man said, "don't condemn the innocent. If
you believe I am guilty, you should pass sentence of me. If
not, you should set me free." Bradford, the well-loved pastor
of St. Paul's in London, was thrown in prison for his beliefs
that differed from the state church during Queen Mary's
reign. While in prison, so many of his congregation came to
visit him that he continued to preach twice a day. He also
preached weekly to the other men in prison, the thieves and
common criminals, exhorting them from the Word of God and
often giving them money for food. Bradford's keepers trusted
him so much; he was often allowed to leave the prison
unescorted to visit sick members of his congregation. All
he had to do was promise that he would return by a certain
hour. He was so careful about keeping his word that he was
usually back well before his curfew.

After a year and a half, Bradford was offered a pardon if he
would deny his beliefs, but he would not. Than after six more
months in prison, the offer was repeated. Again he refused.
"John", his friends warned, "you need to do something to

stall for more time. Ask to discuss your religious beliefs with Queen Mary's learned men. That will take you out of immediate danger". John replied, "If I did that, the people would think I have begun to doubt the doctrine I confess. I don't doubt it at all". "Then they will probably kill you very soon", his friends said sadly. The very next day John was sentenced to death and the keeper's wife came to him with the news: "Tomorrow you will be burned." Bradford looked to heaven and said, "I thank God for it. I have waited for this for a long time. Lord, make me worthy of this"....At four o'clock the next morning, a large crowded had gathered at the place where Bradford was to be burned. Finally, at nine o'clock, an unusually large number of heavily armed men brought Bradford out to the stake. With him was John Leaf, a teenager, who also refused to deny his faith.

Both men fell flat to the ground and prayed for an hour. Bradford got up and kissed the stake itself. In a loud voice he spoke to the crowd: "England, repent of your sins! Beware of idolatry. Beware of false teachers. See they don't deceive you!" Then he forgave his persecutors and asked the crowd to pray for him. Turning his head to John Leaf, he said, "Be of good comfort, brother, for we shall have a merry supper with the Lord tonight!" ("A Merry Supper with the Lord", Jesus Freaks, Martyrs; DC Talk with Voice of the Martyrs).

It was stories of martyrdom like this that I was influenced by as I studied through church history. I cannot begin to convey the direct impact they have had on my growth as a Christ-follower. Stories dating back to the time of Jesus Christ, through the Book of Acts, and the early Church up until today inspire me to live boldly and build up a radical desire within me to proclaim the gospel. As I continued to study both Scriptures and Christian literature, I continually stumbled upon verses and quotes that awakened my passion. Consider the following quotes from the book, A Renegades Guide to God by David Foster, which served to motivate my radical nature- and quite specifically confirmed the thoughts and desires I was struggling with:

> "If I find in myself a desire which no experience in the world can satisfy, the most probable explanation is that I was made for another world"- C.S. Lewis

"Do you have an inner desire to live a free, untamed, bold, adventurous life? One that is exciting, fulfilling, and fun? Do you resist being told what to do or how to think? Do you resent being defined by what you do? And do you gag when people force religion down your throat?"

Finally the book had ended with a link to visit a video, which was the Think Different ad done by Apple, and all of this radically engaged my mind and heart and served as Spiritual confirmation. I was different because I was called to be different, by a Messiah who made me different- hence the term "peculiar people" in Scripture.

In the beginning of 2009, I began to identify the discomfort and stir I had been feeling for the prior couple months, all things were beginning to come together. The fact of the matter is that the Messianic era, the birth and ministry of Jesus Christ, was put into effect so that people might not just live, but to live abundantly, and this would come through seeking His kingdom and His righteousness (ultimately, simply living a life engaged to Him in mind, heart, soul, and strength which would all in all, bring glory to Him). Ever wonder why and how the Kingdom of God was within you yet it was also near? See, Luke chapter 17 verse 12 and compare that with Matthew chapter 3 verse 2.The purpose of the Messiah was to signify the new way that would be revealed and also to create a stir of the Spirit within believers.

That stir was working within me as I continued to seek His kingdom that was embodied within my soul- and the abundance that would come through expressing all things-passions, desires, dreams, and talents- all for His glory!

I was frustrated with big church, all the bureaucracy seemed to get in the way of being disciples. It seemed that the institutional version of Christianity was in direct contrast with the Biblical account of the band of disciples who turned the world upside-down by proclaiming the gospel. In the institutional church my passion and motivation didn't seem to make sense to me or them, but when I read Scripture, my passion seemed to fit perfectly with what Jesus Christ had sought in His disciples and sent them out to make contagious. And it was at this point I decided- I was going to read the book of Acts. Reading through the book of the Acts of the Apostles is a radical revolutionary step in a Believers life. In the Gospels (Matthew, Mark, Luke, and John) you get introduced to this radical rabbi Jesus Christ who claims to be the Son of God, the Way the Truth and the Life, and calls 12 men to Him.

They travel around feeding people, listening to the Rabbi speak, and go on missions with literally nothing but the clothes on their backs- and then...the Rabbi Jesus is killed and the men scatter...then He resurrects and tells these men to Go! (Matthew chapter 28). The book of Acts brings the story of what the Church did after Christ left. Through these accounts we get to see what these should-be confused by witnessing the impossible, yet energized by witnessing the impossible, group of men do to spread this message.
This is the Church in action! As I sat and got engulfed in the story line of the book of Acts, I imagined living that as my purpose and began to commit to the same thing in a 21st Century context.

It is simple. It could be said that I had an encounter with Jesus Christ in Auburn Correctional Facility. Through my studies I had become one of the witnesses because I could demonstrate and explain the "convincing proofs" (Acts 1:3) of Jesus Christ and His ministry. Therefore, I creatively placed myself in the text of the book of Acts (and yes, have yet to return). The prior months of frustration that were going on within my mind, heart, soul, and Spirit began to make sense. I had officially become a "Jesus Freak"! Now just as the Apostles in Acts, I was being sent out with the message of salvation to "this perverse generation". The only thing that seemed to cause more confusion was:

Where had all the Radicals Gone??

" . . . they drew Jason and certain brethren unto the rulers of the city, crying, these that have turned the world upside down are come here also (Acts 17:6)".

After the resurrection of Jesus Christ, His band of disciples, set out defying the religious institution and going against society norms, all in the effort to preach that everyone must "save themselves from this corrupt generation". That is the same message we as the body of Christ need to be yelling today. I sometimes sit and think about the current state of things, are we reading the same Bible about the same followers? This isn't some sit in church, clap your hands, sing a song, listen to a message and live a good life type of thing here, this is the call to be radical. Let us always remember the Spirit of the band of disciples who followed Christ, who we call Apostles. We musn't forget to look to Church history for those who have blazed these trails before us.

The book of Acts is filled with exactly that- Acts of the Apostles. Peter on Pentecost preaching to multitudes, he is warning them and preaching with a passion, that they must realize the Truth. After a great healing, Peter once again preaches about repentance to the onlookers. These two stories alone show a pattern of consistency and passion, so much so that Peter and John were brought up for trial by the religious leaders. Read how many believers were added to the Church! I say that not to point out that we need bigger walled churches, but rather to show that in some senses we have lost the passion for the lost. Only the Spirit of God can give us this radical passion, which will provoke us to get out there and be heard.

If today, there was to be a persecution of Christians in our land, would our testimonies and work shine so brightly that we would be dragged away? I fear not because unlike the Apostles, most of us are not being heard, or shaking things up. The world of the Apostles was made the world uncomfortable while today's Christian enjoys the comfortable "churchianity"; the normal faith of the day. These days everyone claims the title of Christian with no fear of persecution or discrimination.

Polycarp, a faithful disciple of the Apostle John, was an example of a follower who during persecution was singled out and was martyred. This was a man who fought heresies in the Church and dedicated his life to the ministry. Or consider the Monks, such as Anthony or Francis. At a time when the Church was beginning to inter-mingle with the affairs of the world, these monks set themselves apart and fled away from the institutional church. Many of us fail to realize that this upset the "religious world" and Rome had a lot of hostility toward them. Imagine that, the same Church that calls these men "Saints" actually disregarded and persecuted them while they were alive.

> "Constantine adopting the Christian faith resulted in a decline in Christian commitment. The radical believers who Diocletian killed were replaced by half-converted pagans" - Church History Textbook

Another great believer, Peter Waldo (1140-1218) led a band of believers much like the Apostles and is considered to have led one of the first "back to the Bible movements". The Waldenses preached a return to the simple life of the Apostles, living a voluntary life of poverty and preaching. Once again, this radical move challenged the ideas of the day, and therefore was declared heretical and by the 13th Century was pretty much scattered. Even more, let's look at the challenge of John Wycliffe and John Hus, both who are considered reformers of their day. They saw the problems in the Church and rather than sit and complain, they took the initiative to make the necessary changes. Many could question, where would the Church teachings be today if it wasn't for the courage of these two men?

Let's consider the Haystack Prayer Meeting. Which is actually fairly new to me. I have studied Church History for a couple years now, but up until I studied a Missiology course for Bible school, I had never heard of this. Wow, the story of these young men who took another great radical's thoughts (William Carey - Father of Modern Missions) and allowed themselves to be catalysts to bring these ideas to life, is amazing. These students had a divine moment in which they had to consider whether they were going to submit and follow where the Lord was leading them, or give in and give up for the sake of comfort. These ordinary students birthed what we call "Foreign Missions" today.

We all support that, right? Well, here's something to consider: As widely received and welcomed as missions are today, they weren't always.

The book," An Inquiry into the Obligation of Christians to Use Means for the Conversion of the Heathen", was very controversial, yet this led to what we have today. Wow, radical!

"Let me tell you why you are here. You're here to be salt-seasoning that brings out the God-flavors of this earth. If you lose your saltiness, how will people taste godliness? You've lost your usefulness and will end up in the garbage." (Matthew 5:13) The Message

We cannot end a radical essay without mentioning people like John Wesley who led the Methodist Revival and now what we understand as the Evangelical tradition or William Booth who created the Salvation Army.

Or how about the Azuza Street Revival? All of these movements and moments were considered against the norm at that time, but are today, the very driving force leading the Church in purpose and mission. Have we lost the Spirit of revival?

Allow me to conclude with this honest admission. When I sat through the lectures and reading of my Church History class I was so bored and could not wait to be done. But as I would come across some of these men that I've mentioned herein I would get excited and begin "googling more information.

The men of Church History, who were ostracized and criticized, persecuted and condemned, are actually men who have led the Church, the bride of Christ, to be what we are today. Have we lost the passion, the zeal, and the life that will make our mission, the Great Commission, complete?

> "We have sunk into such a compromising way of dealing with the unconverted as to well nigh lost the spirit of the primitive preachers, and hence it is that sinners of every description can sit quietly as they do, year after year, in our places of worship".

> - Andrew Fuller

Since, I claim to be a "Jesus Freak", let us remember and prayerfully consider the "Jesus Freak Movement" of the 1960s and early 1970s. This was a mix of the hippie culture and Protestantism. Now, I am not a hippie, but wow, God is so good, a Jesus Freak is someone who is free to display Christ in the way God created them.

A hippie, a thug, a rock star, a quit mouse type, a Goth, an anarchist, a pretty lady, WE ARE ALL CALLED TO BE "JESUS FREAKS"!!!!"

> Written May 29, 2009 - Mike Miano's personal blog: Freaked-Out Mindset (edited)

Around June 2009, I began to recognize all that was going on inside of me, as I committed to being a Jesus Freak. I realized my ministerial calling was to work with God in creating Jesus Freaks.

A Jesus Freak is simply someone who is called and convinced of the good news that Jesus Christ initiated concerning the kingdom of God, and cannot not help but express it radically, even to the extent of death. I began to bring together ideas for ministry and created Freaked-Out Fellowship. Freaked-Out Fellowship was devised to create a radical band of disciples-outside the confines of denominational ties, outside of rigid religiosity, in an effort to simply infuse passion and calling in the lives of Believers.

I started holding Monday night revivals which would gather at a local park and I would preach messages that would "revive" Believers in radical ways.

I created challenges for Believers who attended and we would commit to getting things done every week- basically to live intentionally on mission. This ministry endeavor has continued up until this day, yet in many different forms. I decided to stop holding the Monday night revivals about a year ago because the passion sort of dissipated in all of us, and I felt the need to humbly learn more about ministry structure (in the book of Acts we learn of a radical band of Apostles just going out, but as the Church grows, we read the Epistles and begin to learn of structure and how that would work without taking away from the radical nature of the Church- there is a lesson in that for all of us).

As far as Freaked-Out Fellowship today, the concept is still alive- and readily recruiting and building up the "royal priesthood", but the time awaits until the Fellowship is in full functioning order and truly "turning the world upside-down" Consider the fact that even Jesus sat and learned until He was 30.

Things take time to come to fruition. God has such an amazing way of dealing with His people. The year 2009 began with some frustrations in ministry and a true seeking of all that desire within me, which I have come to realize, is manifested through the Kingdom of God, in and through the body of Christ (the Church).

In the midst of ministry ideas for Freaked-Out Fellowship, and just discerning life, I began to take on the attitude of not wanting to waste my life.

The kingdom of God sets us up for success in that we begin realizing that all the stuff built up inside us is our equipment to be used and infused with the will and power of Christ alone; we are therefore called to accomplish "greater things". Consider all the things you can creatively imagine that would bring glory to God.

They might seem crazy, right? Well, you are sitting here reading a book by a gang leader turned radical Christian, who believes beyond any reasonable doubt that a man, Jesus Christ, who claimed to be God rose from the dead, showed himself to 11 men, who in turned died for this message, and the movement hasn't stopped since 33 A.D..

Do you see the problem with the popular concept of what is possible?

> "I know what it is to be in need, and I know what it is to have plenty. I have learned the secret of being content in any and every situation, whether well fed or hungry, whether living in plenty or in want. I can do everything through him who gives me strength (Philippians 4:12-13)".

With the concept of not wanting to waste my life, recognizing the kingdom of God within, and the amazing understanding of God's power working on my behalf, I began to dream big! I began to create my bucket list.

Have you created yours? Surely our bucket lists might be different, unless you have aspirations to visit a monastery, fight in a cage match and win, go to church dressed like a prophet, or visit a persecuted Christian country, but ultimately they all bring glory to God, properly submitted and engaged to Him.

Helen Keller once said, "Life is either a daring adventure or nothing at all". Which reminds me of a similar quote by T.S. Eliot, "Only those who risk going too far can possibly find out how far they can go". It's reading quotes like that and reminiscing as I write this book, that I realize how and why I have become so radically engaged to Christ. I even quoted on my blog during the time I was learning about "living to the max", that "this is turning me crazier and crazier".

Allow the thoughts of this chapter, to hit home. Jesus Christ has called us to come to Him and die. The only way you can begin to truly manifest all the things that you dream of, that may seem impossible, is to die to yourself, die to the way you necessarily want things to be. Only then can you approach Jesus Christ to be born again (John chapter

3). Now imagine that you are born again to a whole new way of life; think of the excitement. The movie "Passengers", illustrates this point. When the counselor is speaking with the survivors of the plane crash, there is the one guy who is living crazy jumping off buildings, "borrowing" other people's boats and just overall living on impulse. His response to the counselor? "It's like being born again". Now, my disclaimer is that I am speaking in context concerning following Jesus and to Christ-followers, I am in no way promoting that everyone should just live on impulse, that happens after re-birth into the kingdom of God!

> " . . . May God bless you with enough foolishness to believe that you can make a difference in this world, so that you can do what others claim cannot be done". - Ancient Franciscan Blessing

Chapter 5

DON'T WASTE YOUR TIME: NOTHING ELSE MAKES ANY SENSE

It was around the middle of 2009, that I truly began to feel the delight in the realization of being "born again". Consider the passage of Scripture when Nicodemus asked Jesus Christ about the meaning of being "born again":

> "This is the verdict: Light has come into the world, but men loved darkness instead of light because their deeds were evil. Everyone who does evil hates the light, and will not come into the light for fear his deeds will be exposed. But whoever lives by the truth comes into the light, so that it may be seen plainly that what he has done has been done through God."
> (John 3:19-21)

Life as I knew it and saw it around me (even in religious environments) was beginning to make less and less sense. I began to feel the impulse of living in the light, which makes the contrasting aspects of the world seem utterly devastating. Slowly, this renewal of my mind began to set me up against the "patterns of the world", the only thing that made sense was Christ and Him crucified. 'This good news must be proclaimed to the world, far and near, in order for all things to be made new (and essentially to make sense)'.

As this gospel poured out of my life, it set me up against the world. I had critics of all kinds- those who didn't understand my radical nature of proclaiming the need for all things to be "resurrected", those who were clearly jealous of my lively way of preaching and teaching, even those religious elites who wanted to quell my zealous nature and make it a bit more "normal". Being zealous for the works of God makes other so-called followers seem as if they are doing nothing. They are left with two options- get on the bandwagon of being those who follow Christ with a zeal empowered by the knowledge of His gospel (or) simply make excuses and falsely condemn those who are truly doing it.

Not allowing people to be apathetic in regards to following Christ and failing to make concessions for excuse after excuse we can clearly understand why Jesus Himself was killed!!

This just didn't make any sense!! Why don't people understand where I am coming from? Ahh...it's in the above verse from the gospel according to John- " . . . but men loved darkness instead of light because their deeds were evil". Many people are avoiding the light, and this has created ignorance (ignoring knowledge), therefore zeal based on this ignored knowledge isn't understood and is thrown out as absurd. This is played out through the epistles apostle Paul, a man who was told that his much learning had made him mad/ crazy; we see him burdened to preach the gospel in every way, being all things to all men, (Acts 17 & 1 Corinthians 9:19-23). Paul expressed the importance of getting the gospel message to people by means of persuasion:

> "Since, then, we know what it is to fear the Lord, we try to persuade men. What we are is plain to God, and I hope it is also plain to your conscience. We are not trying to commend ourselves to you again, but are giving you an opportunity to take pride in us, so

that you can answer those who take pride in what is seen rather than what is in the heart. If we are out of our mind, it is for the sake of God; if we are in our right mind, it is for you. For Christ's love compels us, because we are convinced that one died for all, and therefore all died. And he died for all, that those who live should no longer live for themselves but for Him who died for them and was raised again.

So from now on we regard no one from a worldly point of view. Though we once regarded Christ in this way, we do so no longer. Therefore, if anyone is in Christ, he is a new creation; the old has gone and the new has come! All this is from God, who reconciled himself to us through Christ and gave us the ministry of reconciliation: that God was reconciling the world to himself in Christ, not counting men's sins against them.

And he has committed to us the message of reconciliation. We are therefore Christ's ambassadors, as though God were making his appeal through us. We implore you on Christ's behalf: Be reconciled to God ."

2 Corinthians 5:11-20

It was this forceful message that compels and persuades that led to my 'being out of my mind for Christ', the old was gone and the new had come. I remember challenging myself to "be normal" and trying and trying to quell the desire to be like the Biblical prophets but I just could not shake the "new creation".

Contemptus Mundi! (Latin - Contempt for the World) And then I picked up the book, *The Irresistible Revolution*- and all "heaven" broke loose. I kept hearing about this book written by Shane Claiborne throughout my studies, it seemed to be popping up in many areas as something that may interest me. Then I read a story by a man named Brandt Russo who decided to go homeless for a year after reading Shane's book. WHAT!?!? Now, that was a must read! Little did I know that reading his book was going to cause one of many paradigm shifts that would change me for the rest of my life.

Shane Claiborne truly brought the dead American gospel to life in The Irresistible Revolution, and as I read I felt that dangerous impulse of the Spirit just stirring inside of me. This was to contribute to the fuel already within me (the Word of God) and truly set me on the course of revolution- "turning the world upside down".

To be completely honest, at this point in time, the constant aggravation of looking at the world as it was in contrast to what God meant for it to be, looking at the Church and Christians in contrast of what they were Scripturally called to be, and the constant discouragement and harassment of others concerning my passion- was beginning to take a toll on me.

This burden was leading me to a feeling of discontentment and cynicism. Shane Claiborne's words made perfect sense in an effort to relieve this tension:

"There is a movement bubbling up that goes beyond cynicism and celebrates a new way of living, a generation that stops complaining about the church it sees and becomes the church it dreams of. And this little revolution is irresistible".

Shane Claiborne accounts stories of sleeping aside the homeless in abandoned churches and on the streets, living in a leper colony with mother Teresa, going to Iraq as a peacemaker in the midst of war, and this just highlights a few of his chronicles of bringing the gospel of Jesus Christ, the message of reconciliation to the world. The word "wrecked" seems best to sum up how I felt at that moment, but in such a glorious way (visit **wrecked**.org).

It was at this exact moment that I began to think and re-think the gospel and the mission of Christianity. What were we telling the world? Did our message gloriously resemble the glory of God? Was I making it my every effort to display this message, truly maximizing on all opportunities? Shane Claiborne spoke about the gospel message being the proclamation that "another world is possible". I felt truly convicted because this didn't seem to be the message that Christianity was proclaiming from the rooftops. How could I begin to cultivate this understanding and display it?

The gospel or better said, the good news, of Jesus Christ was that this world had it all wrong. Another world is possibly by coming into the light and realizing the truth; then, and only then, can we truly understand life.

Think of all those people who are stuck in addiction, or those contemplating suicide, or even just the average person who is apathetic about life, seeing all things as meaningless. IT IS TO THOSE WHOM WE HAVE A MESSAGE!!.

Thinking this over and over in my mind, I began to express a mindset that resembled the prophets of the Old Testament. Isaiah was given a message from God concerning the destruction of Egypt. He took this message and displayed it by running buck-naked through Egypt as an example of their future demise (Isaiah chapter 20). Jeremiah took upon himself the yoke of oxen to display to Nebuchadnezzar the yoke that God was going to break (Jeremiah chapters 27-28). Ezekiel laid on his side for 390 days and then 40 to symbolize the sins of Israel and Judah. He also ate a special bread cooked over dung to further symbolize the destruction coming upon Jerusalem (Ezekiel chapter 4). These are just some of the examples of men who were inspired by a message from God and who took upon themselves the burden to radically express it, this is the prophetic imagination.

I began to realize that in order to begin my calling as a man of God, God Himself was inspiring me, as He did the Apostles to take responsibility of proclaiming the gospel in ways that would stretch me to exhibit it with all my mind, heart, soul, and strength. This would be done by fully comprehending the gospel of Jesus Christ, understanding the kingdom of God, and beginning to envision the world in this capacity. This was to be reality.

Our lives are continual growth moments. The "iron furnace" did not end at my "salvation moment" back in 2005, but rather our salvation, our growth in Christ, and our love for God and others is continually being exercised and challenged. This growth spurt would be one of many yet to come.

As I contemplate these moments, I am reminded of the vision quest concept that the Sioux Indians practiced.

If you have ever seen the movie 300, it's a concept similar to the Spartan child in the beginning of the movie. Basically a time in the wild to find oneself.

In the Sioux tradition the vision gave a man his power, without it he was nothing. Yet with a vision, he was in touch with the sacred forces.

The concept is that a man must be willing to die to himself in order to find life (Mark 8:34-35). This was that moment in my life, the time when I would truly embrace my calling. The problem was, as if I weren't already in a stand-off with the "world", that now everything was making less and less sense. As Paul said, "To live is Christ, and to die is gain". I was one with Paul concerning that statement because I began to understand what vision was all about. As pastor and author Bob Roberts said, "Any vision that does not require your entire life, isn't a vision, it's just a thought".

And so I prayed, "Father, make me a crisis man. Bring those I contact to decision. Let me not be a mile post on a single road, make me a fork, that men must turn one way or another, on facing Christ in me." - Jim Elliot

> ". . . we need more fools, holy fools who insist that the folly of the cross is wiser than any human power. And the world may call us crazy." - Shane Claiborne

Chapter 6

AWAKING THE SPIRIT OF REVIVAL

"I tell you the truth, anyone who has faith in me will do what I have been doing. He will do even greater things that these, because I am going to the Father. And I will do whatever you ask in my name, so that the Son may bring glory to the Father. You may ask me anything in my name, and I will do it."

John 14:12-14

In August 2009, I began to feel the impulse of revival. Looking around and experiencing the body of Christ, started to upset me in many ways. Why were we not acting in faith? Why were we not acting at all? Faith is what sums up the movement. Faith is the basis of understanding Jesus Christ, yet in our failure to understand and live in faith, we were and many times today still are not experiencing Jesus Christ for who He truly is.

The first sermon I preached at Freaked-Out Fellowship Rally Night was based on the book, Get Out of the Boat, written by John Ortberg. In Matthew chapter 14 verses 22-33, Jesus beckons Simon Peter to come to Him, which would require Simon Peter to literally walk on water. The interesting application of this text is that Simon Peter wasn't sure who the "ghost" on the water was, and therefore said, "Lord if it is you, tell me to come to you on the water". Did you catch that? That text alludes to the fact that Jesus Christ is the type of guy that you would know by Him telling you to do something that would require faith- yes, get out of the boat.

Fact of the matter is that you will never experience God's best for your life until you step out in faith. Although that very faith might just cause you to lose everything or to be radically transformed into someone/ something you never knew or understood. Just ask me, I'll tell you all about it! Imagine Simon Peter after that day, do you think he was ever able to go back to normal? For goodness sake, the man walked on water!

In light of this faith aspect I challenged myself: "What am I doing that I could not do apart from the power of God?" It was at this moment in life that I realized that the body of Christ including myself needed to be revived by falling in love with Jesus again.

Now, let me give honest admission here. I regularly poke fun at the wishy-washy, "boyfriend Jesus" stuff that I see prevailing in the popular consumerist-style Christianity today. I don't mean "blind zeal with song and dance type of love".

I am pointing to a greater love, a love that is based on the knowledge of God, a souled-out love that has seen the alternative in light of the truth, and can sing with David, the psalmist:

> "O God, you are my God, earnestly I seek you; my soul thirsts for you, my body longs for you, in dry and weary land where there is no water. I have seen you in the sanctuary and beheld your power and your glory. Because your love is better than life, my lips will glorify you. I will praise you as long as I live, and in your name I will lift up my hands." (Psalms 63:1-4)

Even in writing this I think: It is truly through knowledge of God, a full understanding of His power and glory, that we become so encouraged and full of faith. I must question, how can we look at the face of God, through our applied understanding and wisdom gained through knowledge and not be utterly amazed, satisfied and in awe?

God's timing never ceases to amaze me. For as I was realizing the need of a faith based on a complete falling in love with the God of truth and the truth of God that I came across a new book on the matter. The next growth spurt would be in relation to "Holy Ambition".

This book by Chip Ingram aptly titled Holy Ambition, had its basis on II Chronicles 16:9:

> "For the eyes of the Lord range throughout the earth to strengthen those whose hearts are committed to Him..." (quoted first part of passage to place emphasis, NIV)

Ambition is defined as desire and determination to achieve success. Now, the usual emphasis on ambition is usually based on selfish motives but this is justly called worldly ambition. Holy ambition, in contrast, is a desire and determination to see God glorified. As John Piper puts it: "God is most satisfied when we are most satisfied in Him", and that puts a magnificent spin on the concept of ambition.

Let us look to the book of Nehemiah, the story of a zealous prophet who desired nothing more than to see God and God's people glorified. This man, Nehemiah, had a broken heart for the city of Jerusalem and for the people of God. He truly desired to see God glorified through what was intended for His glory, His covenant of love with His people. Therefore, being burdened by what had come of Jerusalem and its inhabitants, Nehemiah did all that he could. This consisted of getting permission from the officials, developing his plan-of-action through prayer with God, and finally recruiting the help needed to rebuild the city. This came with many hardships from constant persecution to discouragement, yet Nehemiah was inspired by the faithfulness of God that had been exhibited in the past through the Israelites (read this account in Nehemiah chapter 9). This story is a prime example of holy ambition.

Holy ambition starts with a dislocated heart. Look around, what burdens you about the world today? Find your inspiration. What do you see that inspires you? And finally, develop a radical faith. I have always found inspiration in the statement made by sociologist Margaret Mead:

> "Never doubt that a group of thoughtful committed people can change the world, indeed it is the only thing that ever has".

Developing a radical faith is the direct opposite of having "zeal without knowledge". A radical ("rooted") faith creates a zeal that is empowered by and fueled by knowledge. This type of zeal is eternal. The more knowledge gained, the bigger the spark of zeal and vice versa. It's a never ending cycle. In turn this radical faith that allows for B-HADS. B-HADS are Big- Hairy-Audacious, Dreams. These dreams, or goals, glorify God because they demonstrate faith in God's love and promises.

> "For this reason I kneel before the Father, from whom his whole family in heaven and on earth derives its name. I pray that out of his glorious riches he may strengthen you with power through his Spirit in your inner beings, so that Christ may dwell in your hearts, through faith. And I pray that you, being rooted and established in love, may have power, together with all the saints, to grasp how wide and long, and high and

deep is the love of Christ, and to know this love that surpasses knowledge- that you may be filled to the measure of all the fullness of God. Now to him who is able to do immeasurably more than all we ask or imagine, according to his power that is at work within us, to him be glory in the church and in Christ Jesus throughout all generations, forever and ever! Amen" (Ephesians 3:14-21)

Many times we need to examine and re-examine our "follow-ship" of the Messiah. Are we growing in knowledge and falling more and more in love with God daily? Are we continually being inspired and burdened with dreams and goals to accomplish in an effort to bring glory to God? Many times we get caught up in nonsense that brings us in the opposite direction of finding satisfaction in God. Sin being a prime example, and by sin I mean, that which separates us from the intimate presence and communion with God the Father through Christ Jesus.

Throughout 2009, a group of guys and I were meeting and watching a video series called The Truth Project, produced by Focus on the Family.

These conversations were so encouraging and edifying, and today I am clearly in debt to those men and that time we shared. The Truth Project challenged popular assumptions and placed emphasis on the fact that your faith must be a reality.

"Do you believe that what you believe is really real? Because if you really believe that what you believe is real, then Christians will change the world." Del Tackett, the Truth Project

All this learning, thinking, and conversing throughout these past months was both inspiring and burdening yet I could not take my sight off the seemingly backslidden nature of the body of Christ. How did we not see it? I realized I must begin to dream big, I had already committed to the calling of engaging the world and ultimately turning it upside-down.

Why did we, the Church, have more in common with the Humanist Manifesto than the Bible?

I curse the Edict of Milan! This part of church history enabled a compromise in the Church concerning the mission. Our lack of persecution has allowed us to settle for less than the truth, bringing in doctrines that have allowed for the Church to become complacent and seemingly leading us away from a complete understanding and worldview affected by the glorious gospel.

> "Christianity is at its best when it is peculiar, marginalized, suffering, and at its worst when it is popular, credible, triumphal, and powerful" - Shane Claiborne, Jesus for President

Francis Chan spoke on this concept well when he gave his last sermon as pastor of Cornerstone Church. He used Revelation chapter 21 verses 6 through 8 to demonstrate that there will be no cowards in heaven. Reading and listening to Francis Chan materials (for example, his much spoken of book - Crazy Love), one can easily see and understand his zeal to awaken the Church from spiritual cowardice.

The ancient prophets of Israel dealt with this in times past and were known for yelling and making public spectacles of themselves as they tried to awaken the giant (slumbering sinful Israel). It is through the same zeal that Christians will awaken the Church today. We need prophetic imagination.

Just as Isaiah ran through Egypt naked to demonstrate the judgment upon those people, we need willing Christian witnesses to build up a similar zeal and expression of the message (open air preaching is cool, but for all our sakes- KEEP YOUR CLOTHING ON).

It was only when I saw the complacency of the Church and understood the truth spoken through the Word that I began to live with a prophetic imagination.

November 2, 2009
Notebook Notes

Have we (Christians) compromised the mission? Do we focus on seemingly insignificant things in an effort to avoid having to deal with the real issues (i.e., materialistic culture, apathetic Christianity, lack of persecution, lack of care and concern for the lost, and this new version of the "church")?

Or even worse, do we focus on these things as an excuse/ cover-up for what we have now, all the while not wanting to go back to the likes of the 1st Century Church? Consider all that would change!

I always say "it's not necessarily what you do that is sin, rather what you don't do". Think about the gospel centered life. Is it about being sinless (puritan theology) or rather the good news message of a whole different way of life?

Doesn't Scripture teach us that God will prune us of sin (John chapter 15)? Was 'sinless perfectionism' a focus of the Church in the New Testament? Wasn't it the mission that was always the focus?

What if we began to truly focus on the mission in everything we do, from our preaching styles in church to our everyday conversations? What if we trusted

Christ Jesus with His bride, the Church, and allowed Him to be faithful in pruning us of the sins in our lives? Just think. Maybe our complacency in the mission comes from our diverted attention- sin. I am convinced that it is not a message of 'sinless perfectionism' for which we have had Christian martyrs throughout the centuries. Namely because men/ women of God have continually recognized that the gospel rests on the fact that there is nothing in and of ourselves that enables us to be sinless, therefore we must trust God.

It was at this point in my ever-learning walk with Christ that I was introduced to the missional brand of Christianity. I was introduced to books written by men to the likes of Alan Hirsch who have decided it is time to get back to the primary mission- or as he might say-The Forgotten Ways.

At the end of the book, The Forgotten Ways, Alan Hirsch quotes Bill Easum:

" . . . following Jesus into the mission field is either impossible or extremely difficult for the vast majority of congregations in the Western world because of one thing: They have a systems story that will not allow them to take the first step out of the institution into the mission field, even though the mission field is just outside the door of the congregation."

We, the Church, have the life giving force of the world through Jesus Christ. We have lost this through complacency concerning mission, a selfish focus on ourselves through a man-made doctrine of sinless perfectionism, and other doctrines of men. To be true to the context of this book, I will admit that at the time I began thinking like this, I had yet to realize how far the misunderstanding and misapplication of all that Jesus Christ taught, did, and died for had truly reached. Apathy, complacency, and doctrines of men have yet again affected the people of God- as Mark Batterson put it; we are in a state of spiritual somnambulism (sleep walking).

The next questions would be: how long have we been asleep? How far sleep walking have we wandered away from truth and allowed the doctrines of men to lead us? What would be the basis of the next Christian revival that causes the needed reform in the body of Christ?

> The chief ground
> of gladness and joy is,
>
> When God restores to us
> pure and sound doctrine;
>
> For no scarcity of wheat
> ought to terrify and alarm us
>
> As a scarcity of the word.
>
> - John Calvin

Chapter 7

A BIT CONFUSED
REFORMATION MOMENTS

"Unless I am convinced by Scripture and by plain reason and not by Popes and councils who have so often contradicted themselves, my conscience is captive to the word of God. To go against conscience is neither right nor safe. I cannot and I will not recant. Here I stand. I can do no other. God help me."

- Martin Luther, Protestant Reformer

In 1517, a Catholic priest and professor of theology, named Martin Luther initiated what has been called "The Protestant Reformation". Martin Luther challenged the Roman Catholic Church's teachings and the authority of the pope by teaching that the Bible is the only source of divine revealed knowledge. This led to a reformed concept called Sola Scriptura, Latin for, Scripture alone. Martin Luther challenged many of the teachings of his day and showed that the traditions of the Church were in error and stood in contradiction to the truths espoused in Scripture.

Today, whether we are Pentecostal, Baptist, Anglican, or non-denominational, we owe a great tribute to Martin Luther and the "ever-reforming" principle of the Reformed Tradition. It is with that in mind that I took my frustrations with the complacency of the church and many disagreements in doctrinal matters, and decided to study to show myself approved. I started studying various views of theology and doctrine in the Church, everything from how Calvinism contrasted Armenian theology, to eschatology and soteriology. It proved to be confusing at times, although I was constantly and consistently encouraged by the zeal, courage, and seeking of truth both expressed in the 1st Century Church and throughout the Church reformations.

It was with this in mind that I was able to proclaim "Christianus Sum" (I am a Christian) as a tribute to Christian martyr Polycarp when I spoke at the Faith to Faith conference in January 2010. Having the privilege to stand in front of a group of people and proclaim those simple words that have had the impact of persecution and show the true zeal that is alive in the body of Christ was amazing. It was through the conviction of truth, truth espoused through the Word of God, that Christian men and women have laid down their lives.

The Scripture says that it is by the blood of the Lamb and the word of our testimony that we overcome the accuser (Revelation 12:10-12). That is our foundation. Men and women of God being fully persuaded by truth, not by assumptions but by truth, were willing to die.

Do you realize the implications of that? Are you fully persuaded by truth? There is zeal without knowledge and there is zeal empowered by knowledge, it is important to know which zeal you have. We read about the people having zeal without knowledge in Scripture (Romans chapter 10) and this ultimately leads to a lack of understanding the truth, and quite literally being a hypocrite. Living with zeal without knowledge is easy; it leads to an emotional response based on assumptions, which is exactly what was popular in the Church before the Protestant Reformation. Reformations make people think, and this is usually dangerous because it sets people at odds popular presuppositions. I did not yet realize it, but during the year of 2009 and beginning of 2010, I was being set up to challenge my assumptions and continue to grow more and more in the knowledge of God. I thank God continually for all that He has consistently done to bless me and allow for growth. The providence of God always puts me in awe, adding to my zeal.

At the end of 2009, I was growing closer and closer to the Lord, by challenging my assumptions and preconceived notions. And as I felt my inner theology growing, the outward world again seemed to make less and less sense. Around this time, I had met a man named Alan Bondar. Alan was the pastor of a local congregation, at the time- Messiah Reformed Church, now known as New Covenant Eyes Church. Alan is also the author of the book- Reading the Bible with New Covenant Eyes. God's providence (which is a rather religious way of explaining how God does things His way in His time) is always amazing, and worked mightily through Alan Bondar.

One day as we sat and shared lunch, Alan challenged my view by asking- "What do you believe happens when we die?". This sparked an in-depth conversation about what Jesus Christ came to accomplish, accomplished, and the implications of salvation and redemption. I'll never forget what Alan said concerning the 2nd coming of Jesus Christ:
"The coming of Christ was only visible to spiritual eyes, yet was displayed visibly to the biological eyes of all who had faith that the destruction of the Temple in 70 AD was the event that occurred in conjunction with that coming. The coming of Christ was the return of God's presence to mankind that was lost in the sin and death of Adam"- Excerpt from Reading the Bible with New Covenant Eyes

I had heard of this view before called Preterism. I remember having a meeting a while back, while pastoring the Tribe of Dan Ministry, and having my end times view challenged by-

"what would you say to preterism"? My response- THAT'S CRAZY!! And that was exactly my mindset and response to Alan Bondar.

The troubling aspect of being a studious individual and always wanting to be able to explain and expound on things is that when a statement is made, even if it is ludicrous, it must be examined. I imagine that this is the troubled mind of a reformer. So, I set out to study a bit more and see how, why, and where this odd doctrine and concept that Alan Bondar spoke passionately about came from. (You can read the full email responses between Alan and I in the appendix).

Although a reformer indeed, surely not of this world, I was constantly reminded of my place in the world and had to deal with the routine aspects of relationships, work, school, bills, etc. Ignorance can truly seem like bliss at times, and let me be honest; many times I would pray and seek to be blinded, just to avoid the struggles in my mind and heart. God, please help me become apathetic. Odd, right? It doesn't exactly work like that.

The apostle Paul warns the believers in the Roman church to "never be lacking in zeal, but keep your spiritual fervor, serving the Lord" (Romans 12:11). Throughout the time I have been a Christian many times I have had to sort of fan the flame of my faith that way I would not be lacking in zeal and continue in having a strong spiritual fervor. This is a vital aspect of being Christian and should be conditioned consistently, whether in serving the needy, preaching the Word, or simply edifying ourselves and others through prayer. I sought out opportunities that would "fan-the-flame" in my life and this concept helped me understand what Mahatma Gandhi was seeking when he did his experiments with truth.

Everything from carrying the cross down Cleveland Avenue in Fort Myers to reading Scripture out loud in front of Wal-

Mart had a two-fold purpose. Of course, I desire to preach the Word of God day in and day out, but the deeper motive was for me to utilize these opportunities to serve and grow in zeal for the Lord. In the beginning of 2010, I decided to embark on a bit of an "experiment with truth" exercise in which I would spend the months of January through April understanding different expressions of the Christian Church.

So I set out as a Catholic in January and learned the rosary and attended a local Catholic Church (still have yet to get through the entire Catholic Catechism). In February I attended a Greek Orthodox Church and learned to pray using the khomboskini and read an interesting book about Orthodox, being the only true way to be in Christ Jesus (The Way: What Every Protestant Should Know About the Orthodox Church). In March I visited Reba Place Fellowship which is a new monastic environment to which I traveled by bus from Fort Myers, Florida to Evanston, Illinois dressed like a monk. The trip was fun and I made an Amish friend, and in the new monastic environment I learned how New Monasticism is developing. This exercise was exciting and helped me understand different "brands" of Christianity.

Yet to be honest, this didn't serve to quell the searching desires in my heart and I knew there was much more to be learned and understood about the history and theology of the Church.

In February I attended Alan Bondar's church for the first time and he preached an awesome sermon- "Free to Do What?" which was based on Romans chapter 14. I had always searched for the meaning of the kingdom of God and came across a variety of views, but on that day Alan introduced me to a Scripture that I had never let sink in:

> "For the kingdom of God is not a matter of eating and drinking, but of righteousness, peace, and joy in

the Holy Spirit, because anyone who serves Christ in this way is pleasing to God and approved by men." (Romans 14:17-18)

That was the key! Christianity is about the freedom we have received in Christ due to his fulfilling the Old Covenant with ancient Israel. The New Covenant is not about external religious stuff but rather all about righteousness (Christ's righteousness which is given to us through faith), peace, and joy in the Holy Spirit! Wow, couple that with Matthew 6:33 and our lives become focused. Little did I know, or did Alan know, how much that message would revitalize and renew my zeal in Christ. Talk about God's providence, man oh man, God is good!

The paradigm shift that would be caused by a lot of what Alan said that day mixed with our first meeting and all the things I had been learning as I read would push me closer and closer to understanding how God works in the Church, in the lives of His people, and ultimately how He works in the world today.

Ever wonder what the Church looked like before Constantine? Consider this. . . . "the reformation didn't make a radical enough critique: it didn't go back far enough". - As said by Shane Claiborne

With what I had been learning about this doctrine called Full Preterism and looking at the state of the Church in contrast with all the passion for Christ I had welled up inside my heart and mind, I decided- it is time to start at Genesis and get through to Revelation. And that I did.

"What if we read the Bible without being fed doctrine? What would we get out of it? What would we picture the Church as? What about living as a Christian?"- Francis Chan

Theology is simply developing knowledge of God. As I read through the Scriptures without religious blinders, the story made so much sense and came alive. I felt as though God was no longer this elitist sitting above judging humanity, but rather a loving God who has nurtured His ways into the world, and continues to do so. Although, I had a lot going on in my personal life, I just could not shake the focus on the things of God, I felt torn between my life and my Father's business. This passion just kept getting bigger and bigger.

> "It is not enough to talk about the vision or ministry process from the pulpit. The simple process must be shared at dinner tables and meetings. When people see that it is not just a 'sermon thing', it means more". -Thom Rainer, Simple Church

As the organizer of Freaked-Out Fellowship, I constantly spoke about being passionate about spreading the message of Jesus Christ, and how it needed to be a part of everyday life. The prophets and the first century church made this a reality, and I through my understanding of God was committed to the same. The prophets became a bit of a fascination, and I dealt with the term yet again- prophetic imagination.

The gospel message is that important. I have seen it happen in my life and want to see it happen in every person's life that I come in contact with! The prophets made this happen. They made sure you saw and heard what they had to say, and isn't the message of Christ, which was the full revelation of what the prophets spoke of, even more important?? Therefore, I endeavored to read and be inspired by the prophets from Amos to the prophetess Anna.

> "We need converts in the best sense of the word, people who are marked by the renewing of their minds and imaginations, who no longer conform to the pattern that is destroying our world. Otherwise,

we have only believers, and believers are a dime a dozen now a days. What the world needs is people who believe so much in another world that they cannot help but begin enacting it now" -Shane Claiborne, The Irresistible Revolution

In April 2010, I became fully convinced of the truth espoused in the Full Preterist framework. I committed to Messiah Reformed Church and was ecstatic about understanding God through His Word and coupling that with my Freaked-Out Fellowship ministry views. It was awesome to understand why and how the kingdom of God was a reality and my personal passion for conveying the message mixed very well.

Concrete, passionate, and imaginative, prophetic in its form, prophetic speech is nonetheless "a sharp sword", conveying a vision "designed to shock rather than edify. Moderation is a delusion, and only extremists are in touch with reality". Wow that puts things quite boldly, I mean truly though, How much does this message (the Gospel) burden you or even more just fill you with so much joy you cannot help but be "freaked-out"??

> Here is a quote that confirms my approach " . . . prophetic must be imaginative because it is urgently out beyond the ordinary and reasonable". -Quote from my personal blog

Around this time, I decided I wanted to expand my horizons a bit and commit to a foreign mission. I had studied a lot of about the nation of Israel and all that was going on there, and found an organization-Christian Peacemaker Teams-that seemed to fit the description of what I would see as a Christian mission. The Christian Peacemaker Teams have the strong stance of "Getting in the Way" and are committed to peacemaking efforts around the globe. I saw it as educational, a bit dangerous, and a cause I would be willing to commit to, therefore I signed up for the November delegation. At this point I must admit my personal life was in shambles. It seemed that contemptus mundi (hate for the world) had caught up with me and I was said to be so heavenly minded that I was not earthly good. There were many people who disagreed with my choices in life and how I was leading my life, yet I couldn't shake what I understood to be right. I am a man who makes faulty decisions just as anyone else and at this point and time things were coming to a breaking point.

In retrospect, I see God's providence in all things, and fact of the matter is that God's will is God's will. What happens happens, and in reality there is no room for regret, what if's, or any of that nonsense (yes, I am calling it exactly what it is). So, at that point and time- I began to pray and seek advice of others.

My prayer: God, let your will be continually lived and realized in my life. Lead me in Your way, and break my stubbornness down. Make your will a realized vision in my life.

> "But seek first His kingdom and His righteousness, and all these things will be given to you as well." (Matthew 6:33)

> "A man of knowledge is one who has followed truthfully the hardships of learning, a man who has, without rushing or without faltering, gone as far as he can in unraveling the secrets of power and knowledge".

> - Teachings of Don Juan

Chapter 8

NEW HEAVENS AND NEW EARTH

"The seeker shall not rest until he has found, and he who hasfound shall marvel. He who has marveled shall rule like a king, and hewho rules shall find rest". Clem. Alex., Misc. V.14.96; cf. II.9.45; Oxyr. Papyr. 654, 1904; From the Gospel of the Hebrews.

In November 2010, I set out to work toward efforts of peace in a foreign land and little did I know that my prayers concerning God's will in my life would lead to me coming home to a demolition of all I understood to be my world. I left home to visit a foreign land and returned home to foreign circumstances. As I was still processing what I had seen in order to "Know the Faces" in the Middle East, I was forced to begin processing what was going on in my personal life.

Have you ever noticed that when reading the Apostle John's Revelation it shows that everything is wicked and disturbing, yet at the end you are in the beautiful new heavens and new earth? I believe that is exactly how God works. In our rebellion things will get odd, sad, and disturbed, but when His will is finally revealed and realized in our lives, it becomes something beautiful. Many times I have seen how my prayers have worked out in a clear fashion (that illustrates the importance of keeping a prayer journal), yet this time it amazed me. I prayed, God provided answers. It felt as though God in all His sovereignty stuck His hand into my world and just started breaking the things He didn't want there and placing things there that He did. I asked God for vision and wisdom.

I asked God for insight and blessings and was reminded in prayer of our spiritual father of the faith, Abraham. Abraham had a faith that puts all to shame; it's not about seeing any blessing that makes sense, but trusting God.

I continually offered my life up to God, asking to be cleansed from all things evil (1 John 2:15-17). I offered my life as an incense to God.

It was at this point in time that I felt such a joy in Christ that I had not felt in a long time. In my prayer notes, I recorded this as a sort of Spiritual "high", as I was growing in the knowledge of God and drawing closer to Him, I felt as nothing other than a child of the most high God. He was drawing closer to me and I was drawing closer to Him, by His amazing grace!

> "And we know that in all things God works for the good of those who love Him, who have been called according to His purpose. For those who God foreknew he also predestined to be conformed to the likeness of his Son, that he might be the firstborn among many brothers. And those he predestined he also called; those he called he also justified; those he justified, he also glorified." (Romans 8:28-30)

My prayers were being answered more and more. Understanding of spiritual truths that I had been seeking answers to started to pour in, ever-learning and ever-reforming. For example, understanding the riches in Christ granted through salvation, a long time searching for understanding being equally yoked, and the rest we have in Christ all began to become clear to me. Even outwardly my life was being blessed in many ways. The in and outs of an unequally yoked relationship led me to meeting a woman who was seeking Christ wholeheartedly and was helping in many ways edify my faith. I was finding peace in all things and praising God for it.

"God is most glorified in us when we are most satisfied in him." - John Piper

This, my friends is the New Covenant. Jesus Christ had come to fulfill the old way of doing things and therefore to make all things new. (Hebrews 8:13)

Many people, including a great majority of today's Christians, have not realized the depths of the accomplishments of Christ and what we have received through Him.

The biggest factor is that many Christians are living with false assumptions which lead to false expectations of a coming kingdom. The kingdom that Jesus Christ came on the scene speaking about is here and now, therefore, welcome to the New Covenant, or better said- the new heavens and the new earth.

"Then I saw a new heaven and a new earth for the first heaven and the first earth had passed away, and there was no longer any sea. I saw the Holy City, the New Jerusalem, coming down out of heaven from God, prepared as a bride beautifully dressed for her husband. And I heard a loud voice from the throne saying, "Now the dwelling of God is with men, and he will live with them. They will be his people, and God himself will be with them and be their God. He will wipe every tear from their eyes. There will be no more death or mourning or crying or pain, for the old order of things has passed away." (Revelation 21:1-4)

The new heavens and new earth spoken of here was not to be a faraway fantasy world that we arrive in upon death. Theologically speaking, this text is dealing with the covenant change from the Old Covenant of the ancient Israelites who dealt with God through the body of Adam and therefore lived according to the Law of Moses, and transitioning into a New Covenant in which death and sin (the body of Adam) has been defeated.

> "Did you ever regret the absence of the burnt-offering, or the red heifer, of any one of the sacrifices and rites of the Jews? Did you ever pine for the feast of tabernacle, or the dedication? No, because, though these were like the old heavens and earth to the Jewish believers, they have passed away, and we now live under a new heavens and a new earth, so far as the dispensation of divine teaching is concerned. The substance is come, and the shadow has gone: and we do not remember it." - Charles H. Spurgeon

The New Covenant is glorious (2 Corinthians 3:1-18) and allows us to live our lives without fear but rather live in love (1 John 4:16-21). Praise God!

This is where I am today, as I sit and write this chapter I am living life in the New Covenant as an ambassador of the kingdom of God. Do you not like what you see in the world and cannot stomach to call this the glorious New Covenant?

> "For even if the whole world believed in resurrection, little would change until we began to practice it. We can believe in CPR, but people will remain dead until someone breathes new life into them. And we can tell the world that there is life after death, but the world really seems to be wondering if there is life before death." - Shane Claiborne

Let me propose that we begin and continue to be a people of God, a generative community which grows together in the knowledge of God, working toward making all things new! Be inspired by those who have blazed the trails of our dreams and desires before us and are doing so today, but do not fail to be burdened to do the same.

PART TWO

EMERGING MISSIONAL THOUGHTS

"What if tomorrow someone digs up definitive proof that Jesus had a real, earthly, biological father named Larry, and archeologist find Larry's tomb and do DNA samples and prove beyond a shadow of a doubt that the virgin birth was really just a bit of mythologizing the Gospel writers threw in to appeal to the followers of the Mithra and Dionysian religious cults that were hugely popular at the time of Jesus, whose gods had virgin births?

But what if, as you study the origin of the word `virgin' you discover that the word `virgin' in the gospel of Matthew actually comes from the book of Isaiah, and then you find out that in the Hebrew language at that time, the word `virgin' could mean several things.

And what if you discover that in the first century being `born of a virgin' also referred to a child whose mother became pregnant the first time she had intercourse? What if that spring were seriously questioned? Could a person keep on jumping? Could a person still love God? Could you still be a Christian?

Is the way of Jesus still the best possible way to live? Or does the whole thing fall apart? If the whole faith falls apart when we reexamine and rethink one spring, then it wasn't that strong in the first place, was it?"

- Rob Bell

It has been said that we are on the verge of a great emergence. Phyllis Tickle, Religion Department editor of Publishers weekly and sought after writer/ speaker, explained in her book, The Great Emergence, that this emergence or "rummage sale" happens in all spheres of influence every 500 years and especially in the Church. Marcus Borg, Biblical scholar and distinguished professor of religion and culture , said "the emerging paradigm has been visible for over a hundred years", which he went on to explain as a shift in how we view the Bible and Christianity as a whole. Borg notes the bestsellers of our time and the drastic decline in mainline denomination membership, as a clear appetite among people for something new- something emergent. Also, Franciscan Priest Richard Rohr speaks about the emergence of a new reformation, a reformation that will distinguish itself from all the others by being focused on a positive rather than a negative critique. He said ""The best criticism of the bad is the practice of the better. Don't waste the next 20 years of your life being against anybody, anything, any institution. Just go ahead and do it better".

Emergence or emergent is defined by the Miriam-Webster Dictionary as "arising unexpectedly or a call for prompt action". With a current emergence in Christianity happening we can readily see a reformation on the horizon since there is always an emergence that precedes reformation and renewal in the body of Christ.

For example, in the 14th century, there was a lot of stir about the Word of God being the sole authority in the Church rather than man-made doctrines and hierarchy. A man named John

Wycliffe (1330-1384) started this process by declaring that the Word belonged to the people not just the Church authorities. Three decades later John Huss spoke up for the authority of the Word of God in the Church and was burned at the stake, yet this was still an emergence of what was to come. This emergence led to a reformation in the early 1500's, the Protestant Reformation, when the German priest/ theology professor Martin Luther spoke against the Catholic traditions and man-made doctrines and so began the case for sola scriptura (a Reformed traditional teaching meaning By Scripture Alone). As this picked up momentum in Germany, Ulrich Zwingli started a similar movement in Switzerland which led to the Anabaptist movement, John Calvin's Calvinism, and ultimately what we know as Christianity today.

Are you excited yet? My brothers, sisters, friends and foes this is where we are today in Christianity, it can clearly be seen on the horizon as it has been for a while now. Just like in the Protestant Reformation the emergence and ideas of reform have had their rise in theological circles for a while now, yet we are beginning to see the concepts and ideas trickling into the laity.

The postmodern atmosphere is what has brought about the current emergence. Postmodernism can be defined and explained through the social changes and shifts that we have seen happening beginning at the start of the 20th century. Modernism which had its rise in the late 19th and early 20th century was distinguished by rationalism and secular intellectualism and was affecting everything from art, literature, to common though (philosophy).

The postmodern thought is the experience of a shift in these views, or as post denotes- something that happens after. Within the modernist framework everything was seemingly black and white, right or wrong, and could easily be defined.

Even though the modern era allowed for immense growth in areas that needed to evolve and change- it isn't that simple.

Today, the postmodern atmosphere is categorized by diversity, an unclear definition of "normal", and skepticism toward all things. Interestingly enough, this goes to the extreme that even postmodernism cannot itself be defined.

In the Modern era we saw a lot of reformations and revolts against the common thought, hence the 'culture of death' moniker put on the era by Pope John Paul II. Even with the change things were still seemingly black and right or right and wrong, and Postmodernism would bring about a breaking of the molds. The current trend in American thought is to question everything, and we see this happening on the shelves of bookstores, namely Bestsellers, and a rise in the rejection of the popular notions of things. This is characterized by the rise in conspiracy theories and films such as Zeitgeist. This skepticism and uncertainty has served to bring about the emergent thought.

Emergent thought is exciting because it is what has brought about growth spurts in all things; in this case specifically- the Christian faith. In reformations and revivals of the past, men of God studied the Scriptures, questioned popular opinion, and were disturbed by the apathetic stagnation of the expression of Christ's message- and this brought about change. In the beginning of this chapter we defined emergence as something that arises unexpectedly or a call to action, and that is exactly what emergent thought is.

Within our postmodern atmosphere, an atmosphere of critical thinking and rejection of the popular common thought, emerges thoughts and allows for growth outside the confines of what is usually just accepted without question. In the decade between the early 1980's and 90's a movement of alternative expressions of Christianity began to arise in New Zealand and the United Kingdom. In the United States a similar vibe was being felt by many, and specific groups were seeking to define what was emerging. Would it provide solutions to the decay so prevalent in the Christian expression of faith and knowledge of God?

"You know, when a forester visits a forest to determine its health, she doesn't climb up into the old growth trees. Instead, she gets down on her knees and digs around in what they call the `emergent growth' at the forest floor. In the ecology of the American church, there are lots of organizations who are tending to the old growth trees, but we seem most interested in what's taking place on the forest floor, at the emergent church level." - Brian McLaren

This led to the Emergent Village, also known as the controversial Emergent Church which is taking the lead in dealing with the postmodern world. While traditional church and denominations declare postmodernism and skepticism to be the enemy and evils of our day, the emergent church has created conversations with the intent to learn together as a community in the place of aggressive sermons. They see church assembly as a time and place to sit together to learn and discern through speaking/ listening in a community rather than through unsubstantiated doctrinal assertions and a positioning of the Word of God.

They see the value of the accountability offered by a community as the authority over the Church rather than a system of hierarchy and traditions of mere men. These have been proposed as the solution to dealing with our postmodern society in a Christian context.

In speaking about the emerging paradigm, American Biblical Scholar Marcus Borg wrote, "a way of seeing the Bible (and the Christian tradition as a whole) as historical, metaphorical, and sacramental, [and] a way of seeing the Christian life as relational and transformational".

The "sheeple" aspect that dominates popular Christianity today is namely due to the traditions and doctrines of men that have crept into the Church over time. Instead of compelling and challenging believers to become disciples of Christ, we have enabled a babe mentality that keeps people under the authority of a specific church and/or denominational view.

The encouraging thing is that we are living in the time of the emergence. We get the privilege and the burden of yet again witnessing a critique, revolution, or simple a shift (choose whatever term you may like- I prefer reformation) of the church. Throughout the history of God's people we learn about men of God who challenged the status quo and gave energy to what was about to happen next through the wisdom revealed by God. In the Old Testament we read about social prophets like Amos who spoke out against Israel concerning the injustices they committed against the poor and oppressed, Hosea who laid out the blueprint for Israel to get back to the knowledge of God, and Isaiah who explains the contradictions in the worship of the people and the hypocrisy they display. Yet, in each of these prophetic critiques there is always vision for something new on the horizon when the people repent. The fact of the matter that's revealed by the prophets is that the renewal, or better yet, the healing is going to occur as God wants it to. The question remains: will the people be ready for it?

> "Seek the Lord while he may be found; call on Him while He is near. Let the wicked forsake his way and the evil man his thoughts. Let him turn to the Lord, and He will have mercy on him, and to our God, for He will freely pardon. For my thoughts are not your thoughts, neither are your ways my ways, declares the Lord. As the heavens are higher than the earth, so

are my ways higher than your ways and my thoughts than your thoughts. As the rain and the snow come down from heaven, and do not return to it without watering the earth and making it bud and flourish, so that it yields seed for the sower and bread for the eater, so is my word that goes out from my mouth: It will not return to me empty, but will accomplish what I desire and achieve the purpose for which I sent it." (Isaiah 55:6-11)

The Biblical prophets understood what it meant to receive a message from the Lord and they expressed it with all their energy. So we have heard the story about Isaiah running through Egypt naked to display the message of what God was doing in their midst and Hosea who marries a prostitute to display how Israel had prostituted themselves with other gods rather than the true God.

There are many more Biblical examples of men and women of God who used what Walter Bruggerman has termed the "prophetic imagination". Jesus Christ displayed the same zeal when He spoke out against the hypocritical and disgraceful way the religious leaders of Israel displayed God, and in response Jesus Christ threw a "temple tantrum". (Mark chapter 11)

The Apostles used the same energy, zeal empowered by knowledge, to "turn the world upside down" and therefore the legacy continues as we seek to proclaim the good news of Jesus Christ and persevere with spiritual fervor. This implies that today as Christians, as we grow in the knowledge of God, we will begin to have the same initiative to utilize "prophetic imagination" to display what God is doing. This is being "freaked-out" by the new covenant, and being "freaked-out" occurs when we know what God is doing in our midst, have knowledge of His ways, and seek to express it with all of our mind, heart, soul, and strength, individually and corporately.

In order for the prophets to exhibit the necessary zeal, it was important for them to understand what God was doing and what God was saying, thus the verse- "Be still and know that I am God". In ancient Biblical times, when the Law of Moses was in effect, a prophet could be stoned for giving false prophecy, therefore it was a serious matter to discern the situation, the Word of God, clearly. Today we have the 66 inspired books of the Bible, and plenty of avenues to research through, which leaves us without excuse. When the apostle Paul went to Berea and preached the gospel and explained how the Messiah Jesus Christ fit all the prophecies of the Old Covenant coming Savior, the Bereans searched the Scriptures to see if what he said was true. Where is that "searching the Scriptures" attitude in believers today?

The members of the body of Christ are in dire need of an Elijah moment. In I Kings chapter 19, we read about the prophet Elijah going up to the mountain top and seeking to hear a word from the Lord. Today, we must do the same thing by seeking Him through the Scriptures! As we understand God through His inspired Word and the example of Jesus Christ in the Gospels we will be able to attain a zeal empowered by knowledge to fulfill the role of a Christ-follower in the world.

As we enter the Scriptures with the intent to understand the gospel message (which means the good news of the Messiah) in context and by the blessed understanding given by Holy Spirit, we will develop a better understanding of what the pure and undefiled gospel truly is.

For many this may lead to a paradigm shift, which begins when we start questioning the reality that we formerly understood in light of newer and clearer realities. This will happen many times as you grow in the knowledge of God and it will require dedication to start out with the milk of the Word as a babe in Christ and grow into a mature believer who understands the full scope of the good news that Christianity offers. When

Jesus Christ met with the woman at the well (John chapter 4), He allowed her to be critical and ask questions, which He answered. He then spoke convicting truth to her and gave her the opportunity to repent and experience a paradigm shift. He offered her the good news, the living water that would lead to eternal life. That is the good news of the Messiah, the offer to the world that Jesus Christ died for was restoration into the presence of God, which is exactly what was lost in the Garden of Eden. This is the alternative story that is supposed to be told by those who call themselves Christians.

In the book, Living Mission: The Vision and Voices of New Friars, the following excerpt illustrates how imperative it is for Christians to be telling an "alternative story":

> "Ivan Illich, the philosopher and social theorist, was once asked, "What is the most revolutionary way to change society: Is it violent revolution or gradual reform?" He gave a very careful but very insightful answer: "Neither. If you want to change society, then you must tell an alternative story". The Church has the most revolutionary story in the history of mankind, but for some reason we continually fail to tell it in all its dimensions and to live in its reality. Instead, we settle for alternative realities and lesser visions that in the end fall short of that which God would have for us. Mahatma Gandhi once commented on this when he said: "You Christians look after a document containing enough dynamite to blow all civilizations to pieces, turn the world upside down and bring peace to a battle-torn planet. But you treat it as though it is nothing more than a piece of literature".

Unfortunately, the "sheeple" aspect we talked about earlier in this chapter has allowed for a watered down gospel and the lack of serious study within the body of Christ. This ignorance has indirectly created a distorted, contradictory, and unsubstantiated gospel that has been misunderstood and falsely applied to represent the message of Jesus Christ. The first aspect we must understand when reading the Scriptures whether Old Testament or New Testament is the "audience relevance". Audience relevancy is first seeking to understand how the message was intended to be understood by the people it was specifically intended for. For example when Jesus Christ is speaking the words of Matthew 24, who is He speaking to? The proper context would help us realize that Jesus wasn't a raving lunatic yelling into the sky a bunch of prophecies that had no relation to the literal men standing around Him.

The words were intended for them. Today, we read the Scriptures as fulfilled prophecy and glean wisdom and admonishment to be applied to our lives.

The proposed "Sunday service" of the emerging church is a different style of gathering than the traditional church. In our round table style conversations, which take the place of the traditional sermon-style gathering, we read, study, and exegete Scripture as a community. As we do this we begin to uncover an amazing way of reading the Bible through new covenant eyes.

Pastor Alan Bondar wrote a book about this exact concept and taught about the perspective of Full Preterism. Full Preterism (preterism is derived from the Latin word praeter meaning past or beyond) is the intellectually honest approach to audience relevance in the Scriptures.

The good news of the Messiah was misunderstood in the time that Christ graced the earth with His physical presence, and it continues to be a stumbling block for many today due to faulty understandings, doctrines of men, and the snowball effect of both. Full Preterism introduces the fact that Jesus

Christ came and fulfilled everything He said he would, in accordance with the prophecies, in that generation.

We must not read the Bible today as applying directly to us but rather as the source from which we glean the knowledge of how God works and His will for all things.

Here is an excerpt from the chapter What's In It for Us, in Alan Bondar's book, Reading the Bible through New Covenant Eyes:

> "Contrary to popular belief, the Bible is not a book that teaches about the end of God's dealing with mankind on earth as we know it. It is a book that teaches about how God restored His relationship with mankind on earth as we know it. That restored relationship was completed in 70 AD and will continue with mankind forever on this earth as generations come, and generations go. A common question that is often posed by people who are faced with full preterism is, "What do we do now?" It is a great question that is worthy of an answer. It makes sense to wonder what's in it for us if all the prophecies in the Bible have been fulfilled, right? To begin with, if the resurrection is behind us, what does that mean for us today?
>
> Well, if the resurrection hasn't happened, then we are still under the Old Covenant mode of existence, which means that all we get is death. Many skeptics think that full preterism robs them of their hope that they will be resurrected. But the problem is that a hope in the resurrection demands a need for it. If we want the resurrection to still be future, then we have to be willing to lose our eternal life that God has given to us because in order for there to be a resurrection, there has to be a Hades for us to go to after biological death. Who wants that?

The fact is that now, as a result of the resurrection and the eternal death of Death and Hades, all whose names are written in the Lamb's book of life have eternal life already and get to go to heaven immediately after the death of their biological bodies.

This is really no different than the traditional view on this matter, except that the traditional view is inconsistent as to why we can go to Heaven after biological death. So the Biblical doctrine of full preterism teaches that we have been freed from the sin and death of Adam and have been given the eternal life that comes to us because the resurrection has already taken place. So what's in it for us? Eternal life now!"

The similar thread between the emergent church and the theological thoughts of Full Preterism is that they are met with controversy and heretical undertones because they challenge the status quo and traditions of men that are dominating in the Christian Church.

As we sincerely search for the knowledge of God through the Scriptures there will be questions and challenges to common logic, and contrary to popular Christian thought, this is healthy. Consider the Rob Bell quote at the beginning of this chapter which happens to be one of the most abused and misinterpreted quotes I have ever seen.

Rob Bell simply strikes a blow at what is considered to be a highlight of truth in the Bible, the virgin birth, and everyone goes into a frenzy. Most Christians who have immediately rejected what Rob Bell said cannot stand up to the criticism and defend what they believe or why they believe it. As Charles Spurgeon once said "I believe a very large majority of church goers are merely unthinking, slumbering worshipers of an unknown God."

Whereas most Christians took what Rob Bell said as an attack on Christian doctrine, I was able to look beyond that and consider the challenge. What if our foundations are struck and we cannot defend them, are they sure? The Word of God claims "...God's solid foundation stands firm... (2 Timothy 2:19)", therefore we can enjoy the challenge of critical thinking. It is imperative that we begin to place emphasis on the knowledge of God as an aspect of both salvation and discipleship because our faith in Christ is nonsense if it is not based on the knowledge of God.

Our discipleship can be by a zeal empowered by knowledge, or halfhearted converts who possess zeal without knowledge. True Christianity is zeal empowered by knowledge; the Greek Orthodox Church calls this concept theosis (theoria means knowledge of God) which means that our salvation is determined by our growth in the knowledge of Him. The first chapter of the second letter of Peter we read:

"His divine power has given us everything we need for life and godliness THROUGH OUR KNOWLEDGE OF HIM who called us by His own glory and goodness. Through these He has given us His very great and precious promises, so that THROUGH THEM YOU MAY PARTICIPATE IN THE DIVINE NATURE and escape the corruption in the world caused by evil desires (EMPHASIS MINE)".

Did you realize what that implies? It is through the knowledge of Him that we may participate in becoming more like Him. The truth of the matter is that many within the Church are spiritually sleep walking being ignorant concerning the knowledge of God and this is a threat to a full understanding of Christ Jesus and our purpose of being His ambassadors.

Our slumber, or better said our zeal without knowledge is what has allowed the snowball effect of man-made doctrines, misunderstandings, and false teachings to creep into what is so often misunderstood as Christianity, which in turn creates people who are misunderstood as being Christians.

Granted even outside of the popular "Christian thought", there are many misunderstandings that need to be dealt with to ward off universalism, pluralism, and false teachings, therefore the method we must initiate in dealing with these issues is to grow in the knowledge of God.

There are two main threads of Christian thought that I want to expound upon. These are the very concepts I am seeking to introduce, which I believe when properly understood and applied, will usher us into a better understanding of the gospel. First, in dealing with pluralism and universalism, which seems to bring a sense of unity to the message of Jesus Christ, I want to propose the concept of the Emergence-C.

The second concept I want to explain is what I have termed the "fully effective new covenant", namely a post-70AD understanding of the New Covenant initiated by Jesus Christ, which should bring us into a better understand of what Jesus came to do and thus initiated for us to continue in doing today.

> "As iron sharpens iron, so one man sharpens another." (Proverbs 27:17)

In our modern context there are a variety of views within views and all sorts of beliefs about spirituality. According to Merriam-Webster Dictionary, pluralism is defined as, "a state of society in which members of diverse ethnic, racial, religious, or social groups maintain an autonomous participation in and development of their traditional culture or special interest within the confines of a common civilization". As knowledge increases and people are free to choose what they listen to, believe, or even care to know this will continue to grow. Universalism has become very popular and seems to be a proposed solution against judgmental criticism of religion, race, creed, and so forth, and the basic doctrine of universalism is "whatever way you want to get closer to the divine, is your way, and it's the right way, to you".

Now, any Christian who has ever attended Sunday school can quote:

> "Jesus answered, "I am the way and the truth and the life. No one comes to the Father except through me (John 14:6)".

Clearly, Jesus didn't seem to take an open door approach to things. The problem seems to be a lack of an informed response and boldness to tell someone that they are "wrong" and that the Christian message is the ONLY way. If you say something like that you will simply be called "narrow-minded", and who wants that? Many Christians have settled for a relativist approach and choose not to make such a big deal of the ONLY WAY through Jesus Christ; after all we are commanded to love, right? Well, we can love, and tell the truth in an informed way without relinquishing the importance of Truth. I have heard many pastors refer to the Christian message and thus the Church as being inclusively exclusive. As the body of Christ, we should be seeking to love everyone and include them, yet what makes us exclusive is the truth behind the glorious gospel told, lived, and solidified through Jesus Christ. It does Christianity great justice when Christians exercise their minds, and are able to explain the historicity of Jesus Christ (A great read would be: The Case for Christ by Lee Strobel).

As we begin to understand who Jesus Christ was, we can then begin to understand the purpose of the entire Christian message. Why did Jesus Christ have to come? What did Jesus Christ accomplish? What is salvation? There is clearly a component missing in many of the minds and hearts of men and women who think they understand what Jesus Christ's message was- and that demonstrates the need for Emergence-C. The emergence- C is a term I use to explain how God utilized covenants with people to cause new things to happen (emergence) all in an effort to bring people into relationship with Him.

A covenant is a relationship based on agreement which may or may not have conditions. From the beginning of the Bible, in the book of Genesis God creates a covenant with Adam:

> "The Lord God took the man and put him in the Garden of Eden to work it and take care of it. And the Lord God commanded the man, "You are free to eat from any tree in the garden; but you must not eat from the tree of knowledge of good and evil, for when you eat of it you will surely die." (Genesis 2:15)

The covenant God made with Adam was conditional based on eating of the tree of knowledge of good and evil and when this was broken (Genesis chapter 3) it led to the emergence of new possibilities (Romans chapter 5-6). Adam being the representative of man in covenant with God failed and this led to the understanding of fallen mankind.

We see this further as we read into Genesis chapter 6, where the wickedness of man prevails. God is displeased and we read of His intention to wipe out His covenant people, yet Noah, a righteous man finds favor with God and his family is destined to survive the destruction of the land that will happen during God's wrathful flood. The covenant God makes with Noah is:

> "Then God said to Noah and his sons with him: "I now establish my covenant with you and with your descendants after you and with every living creature

that was with you- the birds, the livestock and all the wild animals, all those that came out of the ark with you- every living creature on earth. I establish my covenant with you: Never again will all life be cut off by the waters of a flood; never again will there be a flood to destroy the earth." (Genesis 9:8-11)

God, by His amazing grace and divine will, calls Abram, later to be known as Abraham, in order to begin the restoration and blessings of all nations through this man of God.

The Lord had said to Abram, "Leave your country, your people and your father's household and go to the land I will show you. I will make you into a great nation and I will bless you; I will make your name great, and you will be a blessing. I will bless those who bless you, and whoever curses you I will curse; and all people's on earth will be blessed through you." (Genesis 12:1-3)

The covenant God made with Abram (Abraham) led to the blessings of Isaac and Jacob (Israel) which would lead to the emergence of the Mosaic Covenant for the Israelites (the descendants of Jacob, Israel). The covenant that the Lord made with Moses was as follows:

"This is what you are to say to the house of Jacob and what you are to tell the people of Israel: You yourselves have seen what I did in Egypt, and how I carried you on eagles' wings and brought you to myself. Now if you obey me fully and keep my covenant, then out of all nations you will be my treasured possession. Although the whole earth is mine, you will be for me a kingdom of priests and a holy nation. These are the words you are to speak to the Israelites (Exodus 19:3-6)".

The Israelites agreed a couple of verses later and this led

to the establishment of the Mosaic covenant which has come to be known as the Old Covenant. Under this covenant the Israelites were commanded to be a set-apart people by whom God's will and prophecy would be fulfilled - restoration of His covenant- redeemed, reconciled, and restored.

God promised through ancient prophets what the emergence through the Old Covenant would be:

> "Nevertheless, there will be no more gloom for those who were in distress. In the past he humbled the land of Zebulun and the land of Naphtali, but in the future he will honor Galilee of the Gentiles, by way of the sea, along the Jordan- The people walking in darkness have seen a great light; on those living in the land of the shadow of death a light has dawned. You have enlarged the nation and increased their joy; they rejoice before you as people rejoice at the harvest, as men rejoice when dividing the plunder. For as in the day of Midian's defeat, you have shattered the yoke that burdens them, the bar across their shoulders, the rod of their oppressor. Every warriors boot used in battle and every garment rolled in blood will be fuel for the fire. For unto us a child is born, to us a son is given, and the government will be on his shoulders. And he will be called Wonderful Counselor, Mighty God, Everlasting Father, Prince of Peace. Of the increase of his government and peace there will be no end. He will reign on David's throne and over his kingdom, establishing it and upholding it with justice and righteousness from that time on and forever. The zeal of the Lord Almighty will accomplish this." (Isaiah 9:1-7)

> "A shoot will come up from the stump of Jesse, from his roots a Branch will bear fruit. The spirit of the Lord will rest on him- the spirit of wisdom, and of

understanding, the spirit of counsel and of power, the spirit of knowledge and of the fear of the Lord- and he will delight in the fear of the Lord. He will not judge by what he sees with his eyes, or decide by what he hears with his ears; but with righteousness he will judge the needy, with justice he will give decisions for the poor of the earth. He will stike the earth with the rod of his mouth; with the breath of his lips he will slay the wicked. Righteousness will be his belt and faithfulness the sash around his waist. The wolf will live with the lamb, the leopard will lie down with the goat, and the calf and the lion and the yearling together; and a little child will lead them. The cow will feed with the bear, their young will lie down together, and the lion will eat straw like the ox. The infant will play near the hole of the cobra, and the young child will put his hand into the viper's nest. They will neither harm nor destroy on all my holy mountain, for the earth will be full of the knowledge of the Lord as the waters cover the sea. In that day the Root of Jesse will stand as a banner for the peoples; the nations will rally to him, and his place of rest will be glorious. In that day the Lord will reach out his hand a second time to reclaim the remnant that is left of his people from Assyria, from Lower Egypt, from Upper Egypt, from Cush, from Elam, from Babylonia, from Hamath, and from the island of the sea. He will raise a banner for the nations and will gather the exiles of Israel; he will assemble the scattered people of Judah from the four quarters of the earth. (Isaiah 11:1-12)

"Here is my servant, whom I uphold, my chosen one in whom I delight; I will put my Spirit on him and he will bring justice out of the nations. He will not shout or cry out, or raise his voice in the streets. A bruised reed he will not break, and a smoldering wick he will not put out. In faithfulness he will bring forth justice;

he will not falter or be discouraged till he establishes justice on the earth. In his law the island will put their hope. This is what God the Lord says- he who created the heavens and stretched them out, who spread out the earth and all that comes of it, who gives breath to its people, and life to those who walk on it: "I, the Lord, have called you in righteousness; I will take hold of your hand. I will keep you and make you to be a covenant for the people and a light for the Gentiles, to open eyes that are blind, to free captives from prison and to release from the dungeon those who sit in darkness. I am the Lord; that is my name! I will not give my glory to another or my praise to idols. See, the former things have taken place, and new things I declare; before they spring into being I announce them to you." (Isaiah 42:1-9)

"I revealed myself to those who did not ask for me; I was found by those who did not seek me. To a nation that did not call on my name, I said, `Here am I, here am I'. All day long I have held out my hands to an obstinate people, who walk in ways not good, pursuing their own imaginations- a people who continually provoke me to my very face, offering sacrifices in gardens and burning incense on alters of brick; who sit among the graves and spend their nights keeping secret vigil; who eat the flesh of pigs, and whose pots hold broth on unclean meat; who say, `Keep away; don't come near me, for I am too sacred for you!' Such people are a smoke in my nostrils, a fire that keeps burning all day. See, it stands before me: I will not keep silent but will pay back in full; I will pay it back into their laps- both your sins, and the sins of your fathers, says the Lord.

Because they burned sacrifices on the mountains and defied me on the hills, I will measure into their laps the full payment for their former deeds. This is what the Lord says: "As when juice is still found in a cluster of grapes and men say, `Don't destroy it, there is still some good in it, so will I do on behalf of my servants; I will not destroy them all. I will bring forth descendants from Jacob, and from Judah those who will possess my mountains; my chosen people will inherit them, and there will my servants live. Sharon, will become a pasture for flocks, and the Valley of Achor a resting place for herds, for my people who seek me. But as for you who forsake the Lord and forget my holy mountain, who spread a table for Fortune and fills bowls of mixed wine for Destiny, I will destine you for the sword, and you will all bend down for the slaughter; for I called you but you did not answer. I spoke but you did not listen. You did evil in my sight and chose what displeases me.

Therefore this is what the Sovereign Lord says: "My servants will eat, but you will go hungry; my servants will drink, but you will go thirsty; my servants will rejoice, but you will be put to shame. My servants will sing out of the joy of their hearts, but you will cry out from anguish of heart and wail in brokenness of spirit. You will leave your name to my chosen ones as a curse; the Sovereign Lord will put you to death, but his servants he will give another name. Whoever invokes a blessing in the land will do so by the God of truth; he who takes an oath in the land will swear by the God of truth. For the past troubles will be forgotten and hidden from my eyes. Behold, I will create a new heavens and a new earth. The former things will not be remembered, nor will they come to mind. But be glad and rejoice forever in what I will create, for I will create Jerusalem to be a delight and its people a joy. I will rejoice over Jerusalem and take delight in my people; the sound of weeping and of crying will be heard in it no more. Never again will there be an infant who lives but a few days, or an old man who does not live out his years; he who dies at a hundred will be thought a mere youth; he who fails to reach a hundred will be considered accursed. They will build houses and dwell in them; they will plant vineyards and eat their fruit. No longer will they build houses and others live in them, or plant and others eat. For as the days of a tree, so will be the days of my people; my chosen ones will long enjoy the works of their hands. They will not toil in vain or bear children doomed to misfortune; for they will be a people blessed by their Lord, they and their descendants with them. Before they call I will answer; while they are still speaking I will hear. The wolf and the lamb will feed together, and the lion will eat straw like the ox, but dust will be the serpent's food. They will neither harm not destroy on all my holy mountain" says the Lord." (Isaiah chapter 65)

"The days are coming" declares the Lord, "when I will plant the house of Israel and the house of Judah with the offspring of men and of animals. Just as I watched over them to uproot and tear down, and to overthrow, destroy and bring disaster, so I will watch over them to build and to plant", declares the Lord. In those days people will no longer say, "The fathers have eaten sour grapes, and the children's teeth are set on edge'. Instead, everyone will die for his own sin; whoever eats sour grapes- his own teeth will be set on edge. "The time is coming", declares the Lord, "when I will make a new covenant with the house of Israel and with the house of Judah. It will not be like the covenant I made with their forefathers when I took them by the hand to lead them out of Egypt, because they broke my covenant, though I was a husband to them, declares the Lord.

This is the covenant I will make with the house of Israel after that time, declares the Lord. I will put my law in their minds and write it on their hearts. I will be their God and they will be my people. No longer will a man teach his neighbor, or a man his brother, saying `Know the Lord', because they will all know me, from the least of them to the greatest', declares the Lord. For I will forgive their wickedness and will remember their sins no more ."(Jeremiah 33:27-34)

Jesus Christ, the Savior (Mark 1:14-15) came to initiate the awaited kingdom of God spoke of by the ancient prophets (Matthew 13:17; Luke 16:16; Hebrews chapter 8). The kingdom of God was the fulfillment of the Old Covenant which through judgment and redemption led to the emergence of eternal life in the New Covenant (John 17:3; Romans chapter 8; Revelation 21:4).

God utilizes covenants because it expresses Him as Father, Son and Spirit as relating to the world. All things are done by God for His glory and covenants allow for His glory to be revealed to and through us, as well as giving us the freedom we want and accountability we need. The Old Covenant given to Israel was a matter of works and obedience (Exodus 19:5-8) and this emerged into the New Covenant (Galatians chapter 3 explains this very well).

The New Covenant was the restoration of all things that were lost by Adam in the Garden of Eden (! John 3:8). The Old Covenant was temporarily filling in for and leading up to the New Covenant (Hebrews chapter 10).

"The doctrine of the covenant lies at the root of all true theology. It has been said that he who well understands the distinction between the covenant of works and the covenant of grace, is a master of divinity. I am persuaded that most of the mistakes which men make concerning the doctrines of Scripture are based upon fundamental errors with regard to the covenant of law and of grace. May God grant us now the power to instruct, and you the grace to receive instruction on this vital subject." -Charles H. Spurgeon

Understanding that God deals with us through the New Covenant should lead us into wanting to know more about God and how this new covenant works, and that is why all of a sudden I am seemingly citing a million and one Bible verses. The Biblical covenants of God are hardly understood by many mainstream Christians and are absent from many denomination's theological views. Therefore it is understood why many so-called Christians haven't even grasped the reality and substance of the good news of Jesus Christ that is clearly explained throughout the Scriptures.

Many Christians have a faulty view, or rather an unbiblical one, concerning the effect and consummation of the New Covenant due to a lack of contextual study and understanding of the covenants of God. This is where I will hopefully help by introducing the concept I have termed -"Fully Effective New Covenant". My goal is to utilize this concept to help other believers understand what the true glory of being in the New Covenant. I hope to do so by expounding on in context prophecies and understanding of the Scriptures.

I have spoken a bit about this in previous chapters so I am not looking to provide a detailed analysis (of which one could compile a book in and of itself about), instead I am just seeking to introduce the concept that we need to grasp. Maybe, this will initiate conversation between you and me, you and others, or quite possibly you may invite me to speak to you and others to further expound on this concept. When Jesus Christ resurrected, He sent the apostles out to fulfill the great commission (Matthew 28:16), this was prophetic in order to bring about the consummation of the kingdom of God. If you read the New Testament, you will inevitably realize the urgency of the Coming of the Lord that is continually mentioned.

Today, we see the same urgency expressed in Christians who are waiting for the world to end so that we can be eternally with the Lord. And this goes without realizing the prophecies are 2,000 years removed from their proper context and is intellectually damaging to the Scriptures. The hypocrisy (intellectual dishonesty) and ignorance is, at many times, too much to bear. So, let's consider yesterday and understand the fulfilled perspective.

Contrary to popular Christian thought there is nothing to wait for anymore. Full Preterism is the coined term for the spectrum of theology that explains fulfilled Bible prophecy, and it seems to be the only teaching that allows for context to take place. The Israelite people (as well as all mankind) suffered from the sin-death of Adam and were thus distinguished as being the `body of Adam'. Remember the covenants- Israel was chosen by God to be the priests of God and would be His people only through obedience (Deuteronomy chapter 28). Throughout the prophets we read about the distress and calamity that came as a result of the breach of covenant by Israel, and their perpetual failure at righteousness (Isaiah 64:6). Destruction and Judgment may seem cruel and futile, but it actually demonstrates the wisdom of God because it allowed man to see through the example of Israel that it is impossible to be righteous on our own, thus paving the way for the needed Messiah. The Law of Moses, also referred to as the Old Covenant, would be the schoolmaster in showing our need to embrace a provided righteousness through Jesus Christ (Galatians chapter 3). The righteousness provided through the Messiah in the Messianic age was to overcome the sin-death of Adam that occurred in the Garden of Eden. The ancient prophets of Israel spoke of a time when what was lost in Adam, the Hope of Israel, would finally be restored. This was not to be a Disneyland style Heaven and Earth where we would drink milk and honey all day while floating on clouds and listening to our favorite Christian bands playing live in concert (Be serious . . . isn't that much of what we hear about this place called Heaven that everyone is so excited for?). The Hope of Israel (Acts chapters 24-28) was to be resurrected from the sin-death that was received in Adam, being fully restored into the presence of God without the need for sacrifices and religious regulations, being truly free to live (Check out my blog post in the appendix titled: Free to Live).

Prophecy places judgment and resurrection together (Daniel 12 cf. Matthew chapter 24). God utilized judgments throughout the Old Covenant to teach people righteousness (Isaiah 26:9), and therefore Jesus Christ prophesied the same thing to happen before the New Covenant became fully effective. (Matthew chapters 21-25) Popular eschatology (end-time study) has placed the judgment and resurrection as 'end of the world events' clearly taking the importance of audience relevance away from the text and creating many misunderstandings of prophet terms such as "coming of the Lord", "clouds", "resurrection of the dead" as well as various other terms.

Jesus Christ spoke about the judgment upon those under the Old Covenant which would lead to the Old Covenant becoming obsolete and this judgment would bring about the everlasting covenant (Hebrews 13:20-21). The judgment which happened in 70 A.D. upon the temple and the Old Covenant people in Jerusalem was the fulfillment of what Jesus Christ predicted. The judgment upon Jerusalem brought about the destruction of the temple made with hands (Acts 7:48), at which the Lord and His people would serve as the temple of God (Revelation 21:22). The Old Covenant temple demonstrated the strength of the Old Covenant and the divide between God and man which when destroyed brought about the presence of God with man.

Destruction of the temple of sacrifice showed how Jesus Christ's death, burial and ascension completed the sacrifices for righteousness once and for all . . . At the judgment in 70 A.D. the eternal destiny of all people was finalized- either eternal life or death, which led to the resurrection of those in Hades and ultimately a throwing away of Hades. The implications of a past fulfillment of the Day of Judgment are enormous. Many Christians, as I once did, look to a future time when everyone will stand before a great big throne of God and be judged one by one.

Ideally, this sounds great, kind of scary, yet helps us explain with urgency why people must choose Jesus Christ. Yet through study and intellectual honesty, many will realize this is not what is depicted through the text. The glory of the New Covenant is that we cannot be judged (John 3:18 and Romans 8:1).

If you study and allow for the Scriptures to shape your view you will inevitable realize the context of the Messianic age in the first century. Simply read the gospels of Matthew, Mark, Luke and John- salvation, eternal life, immortality, and all the riches of Christ expressed through the New Covenant are maximized at the completion of prophecy- this was the hope of Israel. But in order to understand the hope of Israel, one would have to study the Old Testament to see what led up to the culmination.

"And I heard a loud voice from the throne saying, "Now the dwelling of God is with men, and he will live with them. They will be his people, and God Himself will be with them and be their God. He will wipe every tear from their eyes. There will be no more death or mourning or crying or pain, for the old order of things has passed away". He who is seated on the throne said, "I am making everything new!". (Revelation 21:3-5)

In the Old Covenant God dwelt in the Holy of Holies and did not dwell among man. Today as Christians we recognize that God is among us as we live to be people marked by His presence. If you study the Old Testament prophets, you will see the importance of God to be calling us His people- this was a declaration that God is on our side! In the New Covenant we recognize the tears, pain, and sorrows that had to do with the things of the Old Covenant- sacrifice and regulation, abode in Hades, and waiting for something better.

The fully effective New Covenant brings about eternal life therefore no more death, the sacrifice and regulations have found completion in Christ, and those waiting for resurrection from the body of Adam and the abode in Hades have been set free to experience eternal life in Christ. Realizing our standing with God and that we are now living in the completion of all that Jesus Christ came to establish should invigorate us Christians, to then bring the knowledge of God into all situations. Many Christians are seeing the need, and calling for us to become, a people distinguished by mission, men such as Alan Hirsh, Gabe Lyons, and many others. It is time we answer the call! The fact remains that our theology must be consistent with our understanding. As Romans 14:17 says:

"The kingdom of God is not a matter of eating and drinking, but of righteousness, peace, and joy in the Holy Spirit because anyone who serves Christ in this way is pleasing to God and approved by men".

Due to our faulty understandings we have lost hold of both the Jesus Christ of the Gospels and very much of the Gospel itself, being the good news that Jesus Christ came to speak, express, and even die for. The emergence happening in our society, allows for those who call themselves Christians to be recalibrated. As Alan Hirsch puts it- we need to "ReJesus". As in all times of change, God is going to have His way; the call of reform is going on and will be maximized as we grow in the knowledge of God. After all, even the gates of Hades could not prevail against the Church (Mathew 16:18).

In 137 A.D., Aristides of Athens, a Greek Christian, wrote a letter to the Emperor describing the Christians:

> "It is the Christians, O emperor, who have sought and found the truth. We have realized it from their writings; they are closer to the truth and to a right understanding than all the other peoples, for they acknowledge God. They believe in him, the creator and builder of the universe, in whom all things are and from whom everything comes. They worship no other god. They have his commandments imprinted on their hearts. They observe them because they live in the hope and expectation of the coming age of the world. They do not commit adultery. They do not live in fornication. They speak no untruth.
>
> They do not keep for themselves the goods entrusted to them. They do not covet what belongs to others. They honor father and mother. They show love to their neighbors. They pronounce judgments which are just. They do not worship idols in human form. They do not do to another what they would not wish to have done to themselves. They do not eat the food sacrificed to idols, for they are pure. They speak gently to those who oppress them, and in this way they make them their friends . . ."

Oh, how I aspire to witness and to be a card- carrying member of a Christian community that lives up to that example! This clearly shows what should be the outpouring if we have a firm understanding of Jesus Christ as Lord and Savior.

> "The way forward is going to require something bigger than any one group, including Emergent. I believe that is the postmodern world, truth and power are widely distributed. What I am hoping to see is a network of collaborative networks-maybe like birds feeling the urge to migrate north at the same time because they all sense the same smell of springtime in the air. I am quite certain Emergent will be one little flock in that migration. I hope all of us who are catching that scent can migrate together, guided by the True North of Jesus, the Gospel and grace"- Brian McLaren

Christian brothers and sisters, we are called to be ambassadors for Christ (2 Corinthians 5:20) and commanded to walk worthy of our calling (Ephesians 4:1-16).

An ambassador is someone who is placed in a foreign location to represent the nation they are from. This is a responsibility given to men and women of respect and knowledge who are able to be assigned certain duties of diplomacy. It is our duty to know the truth of the gospel, live lives that exemplify it, and ultimately be representatives in all spheres of life to simply- bring all thoughts captive to Christ. (2 Corinthians 10:5) Let the emerging reformation's call be "Many have 'zeal without knowledge', it is time that we stand our from the crowd being known as those people who have "zeal empowered by knowledge". This is the reformation that is emerging, and which will call all things to the light. Examine yourself to see if you are in the faith (2 Corinthians 13:5). Spiritual fervor will be the mark of those who have their discernment exercised (Romans 12:11). Don't be left behind!

PART THREE

TEOTWAWKI
GOING BACK TO THE FUTURE

I hope you have been empowered by the knowledge espoused throughout this book. If so, I pray that it will lead to the end of the world as you know it. We must begin to have a healthy sense of contemptus mundi (hatred for the world) and seek to see all things restored- with the intent to bring glory to God!

In 70 A.D. the Jewish temple was destroyed and this was an end to the Old Covenant world, where the temple was the center of life. The Old Covenant age (Greek term- aion) was ended and led to the emergence of the New Covenant age. The eternal age (Hebrews 13:20 & Ephesians 3:21). Imagine being an Jew alive at the time that the destruction of Jerusalem occurred in 70 A.D., visibly the times were changing and it was happening fast, making the words of Jesus Christ ring very true (Matthew chapters 23-24 & specifically Luke 21:20-22).

> "And this seems to me to have been the reason why God, out of his hatred of these men's wickedness, rejected our city; and as for the temple, he no longer esteemed it sufficiently pure for him to inhabit therein, but brought the Romans upon us, and threw a fire

upon the city to purge it; and brought upon us, our wives, and children, slavery, as desirous to make us wiser by our calamities" -J osephus, Jewish historian, The History of the Destruction of Jerusalem, Book XX Chapter VIII Section 5

Due to the failure of applying audience relevance to the Biblical text and realizing what it meant to the people to whom the words were spoken, to whom the Biblical letters were written, and how it all applied, we are missing a great agent of change that occurred in transition from the old to the new. The lack of proper exegetical application of the New Covenant that Christ came to initiate forces a frustration on us much like that which plagued Michael J. Fox in the movie Back to the Future. Our failure to properly understand where we are today in terms of Biblical prophecy leaves us waiting for certain things to happen that will not, and has us preaching a message that pertained to the first century generation. Therefore we stay stuck in a past time frame without realizing what we are losing out on and failing to live in the life that was given to us through fulfilled prophecy.

You shall know the truth and the truth shall set you free (John 8:32). The truth when properly applied in context, will serve as our equivalent to Michael J. Fox's flux capacitor and will free us from man-made doctrines and enable us to get back to where we belong- living in the New Covenant!

Applying "audience relevance" to the Holy Scriptures allows us to begin to notice the context of statements such as "the end of the world/age", "about to come", and many other audience related Scriptures.

For example, in Matthew 24, Jesus Christ is telling the disciples of the impending judgment that will occur on the Temple and He tells them of the signs of that will occur prior to its happening and when the end will come (Matthew

24:14). The end of what? The end of the world? I propose that audience relevance helps us to realize it was the end of the Jewish temple age- the Old Covenant- which brought about the New Covenant Age.

This understanding changes things quite a bit. Have you been looking around and waiting for the end to come that way things will get better? Have you been looking for some future event that will change everything? Fact of the matter is- EVERYTHING HAS BEEN CHANGED IN 70 A.D. The transition from death to life already happened. The presence of God has been restored. The kingdom of God is ever increasing and will never end. So what now?

How would you define your life right now? What takes precedence over everything else? Could you say "to live is Christ and to die is gain (Philippians 1:21)"? Are you living in the complete satisfaction and understanding of all that Christ accomplished and therefore have received your rest (Matthew 11:28)? Are you trusting in the promise told to the disciples and of which also rings true for us today:

> "Seek first the kingdom of God and His righteousness
> and all these things shall be added unto you."
> (Matthew 6:33)

If not, I extend the same call that was imposed on the Jews in 70 A.D. - End Your World! Realize where you stand in life and how much that pales in comparison to what God is doing in the world, and ultimately what He can do with and through you once you realize the bigger picture. Coming to the knowledge of God and the realization of His Truth is not a judgment on your life, as it seems many Christian leaders have made it to be, rather it is a blessing and an upgrade .

"It starts with rediscovering the full story of the Gospel, which leads them to recalibrate their conscience to allow them to be in the world, which forces them to rethink their commitment to one another and their neighbors, which inspires them to re-imagine a renaissance of creativity, beauty, and art that the world hasn't seen in centuries, which culminates in redeploying the church where the world needs it most (Gabe Lyons, The Next Christians, page 66)".

The emergence is happening!!!

Applying "audience relevance" to what Jesus Christ spoke concerning the judgment of Israel happened in 70 A.D. allows for us to glean wisdom and application for our lives. The world that the Jews knew to be there reality was ended and therefore brought about the greater purpose of God. That could be quite possibly what is going on in your life right now!!

I challenge you- end your world today! Begin to see things through the lens of God and allow for the greater things to come to fruition in your life.

> "I tell you the truth, unless a kernel of wheat falls to the ground and dies, it remains only a single seed. But if it dies, it produces many seeds. The man who loves his life will lose it, while the man who hates his life in this world will keep it for eternal life. Whoever serves me must follow me: and where I am, my servant will also be. My Father will honor the one who serves me." (John 12:24-26)

PART FOUR

CONCLUDING THOUGHTS

Today, many Christians who recognize the apathetic institutionalized form of religion being passed off as Christianity quote the popular phrase-"We are called to make disciples, not converts". Unfortunately this makes it all too clear that the large majority of so-called Christians are "altar call" converts with no true discipleship in their lives.

Many churches have initiated discipleship programs and concepts to fill in the gap between conversion and life in Christ, yet this still does not allow for the natural outpouring that comes from being covered in the dust of the Rabbi.

As I sit and ponder what I want the reader to conclude with, I contemplate my calling and what I see emerging. I am called, as I hope many will begin to see in themselves, to make disciples who make disciples. I am known for saying, "I am called to create Jesus Freaks", which pretty much means to create disciples of Christ who are so in awe and passionate about the gospel that they freak-out.

Imagine winning the lottery. We both know that if we won that 70 Million we would be so excited; making sure everyone on Facebook knew, as well as everyone we came in contact with, and we would definitely be reaping the reward of instant riches. Right? Why can't we realize how much of a reward and how exciting the grace of God truly is? Quite possibly the lack of an authentic knowledge of God is the answer.

I hope that as you read through my story you were convicted to think through yours. After all, the Scriptures state that we overcome by "the blood of the Lamb and the word of their testimony". I have written this book with loving criticism of what the institutional church has offered as the gospel of Jesus Christ, the man-made doctrines, and overall the way Christianity is lived out, as well as my ideas of how we can get out from under this mess. We must remind ourselves, as St. Augustine said, "The Church is a whore but she is still my mother". The glimmer of hope is the emerging reformation.

As I end this book, I want to leave some examples of lives lived for the glory of God alone, in hopes that you, through my story and theirs, who will pick up the mantle and die, so that Christ may live. It's imperative that you be inspired or challenged by this book; we are all called to be agents of change for the emerging reformation, in one way or another.

Recently, Quanti (my soon to be bride) asked me what I feel born again Christians should look and live like. I began to describe traits such as being convicted by truth, zealous to defend the gospel and Biblical truth, loving others, and possessing the desire to be missional and spread Christianity by word and deed. Quanti then said something that created a sort of mental breakthrough for me- "Oh, so pretty much if Martin Luther and Mother Teresa had a baby?". Obviously, we are not talking a biological baby, but rather an ideological baby; a mix between the stance of truth that initiated the Protestant Reformation and the dedication of one of the most selfless loving people to grace this planet.

I realize that it is through stories (testimonies) that we get a glimpse into what Christianity looks like lived out. Over the years I have read many autobiographies and biographies that have encouraged me. It's these stories that bring messages to life. As I sit through a church service, I take notice of the evangelistic message that is preached from the pulpits Sunday after Sunday (something we have gleaned from the revivals during the Great Awakening), yet we have allowed these revival messages to take center stage over the communal discipleship style of the early church.

We no longer find it necessary to know and understand the gospel message in effort to spread it to the world; we simple invite our friends and family to hear it presented by the pastor on Sunday. We no longer find the need to be intentionally missional in engaging the world because our goal is to invite our friends and families to Church (and we don't want to force our religion on other people or force ourselves out of our comfort zones). So, now what?

Do we just go back to our mediocre lives and do this again next Sunday? Have church gatherings simply become social clubs with social events?

Ever wonder what a Sunday service would look like if we all were presenting the gospel and bringing people closer to an understand of the Lord in our own lives rather than bringing them to hear the evangelistic message presented on Sunday? We could then focus our Sundays on hearing stories that will encourage us to be more missional.

We could then strategize how to best "turn the world upside down" and we could simply spend time fellowshipping in unity and love.

Allow me to share some of the stories of men and women who challenged the status quo in the Christian Church who weren't willing to just "go along to get along". They saw the need to do something. Hopefully, their stories will add insight into what we need to be doing today as the reformation emerges. Since I already detailed the life of Martin Luther in this book, I will just point out some of the fundamentals. Martin Luther risked everything, his position in the Catholic Church and his life, and had to go into hiding because he was convicted of truth outside the bounds of what was being taught. The Protestant Reformation was initiated by a man who read the Scriptures and saw contradicting teachings being taught to the common people.

What did Martin Luther do? He set out to teach what he had learned through the Scriptures and challenged the popular teachings of the day that went against the truth. He published writings to further spread the truth of what the Scriptures said. Martin Luther's proclaiming and discerning the truth caused a split in all that he had ever known as home- the Catholic Church.

Martin Luther did not want to cause a division, rather he just wanted to challenge the false teachings that were so prevalent in his time, and foster efforts to bring the Church back to Scriptural truth. Today, what many of us know as Christianity was birthed through Martin Luther's' courageous reforms. As a self-proclaimed reformer, known in some circles as a heretic, I can tell you how hard it truly is to go against the popular thoughts of the day, but in the end of the troubles, how important is truth to you?

Let us begin to search the Scriptures to know the truth and have the courage to stand against man-made doctrines that water down and change the Word of God. As Martin Luther said at the Diet of Worms:

> "Here it is, plain and unvarnished. Unless I am convicted [convinced] of error by the testimony of Scripture or (since I put no trust in the unsupported authority of Pope or councils, since it is plain that they have often erred and often contradicted themselves)

by manifest reasoning, I stand convicted [convinced] by the Scriptures to which I have appealed, and my conscience is taken captive by God's word, I cannot and will not recant anything, for to act against our conscience is neither safe for us, nor open to us. On this I take my stand. I can do no other. God help me. Amen".

When searching for someone who applied as much of a conviction in matters of Scripture to living a Christian life we find no better example than Dietrich Bonhoeffer. Bonhoeffer challenged the Christian Church in regards to developing a theology that naturally flowed into an active Christ glorifying lifestyle. As a pastor and theologian in Germany during the Third Reich of Adolph Hitler, Dietrich Bonhoeffer saw that the social atmosphere resembled what he called "the world come of age" and thus the solution would be a "religionless Christianity". The world come of age was explained by Bonhoeffer as a time when mankind had become independent thinkers and had begun to reject God because it seemed He was no longer needed. The religious institution would see it fit to continually force the logical mindset of mankind into adolescence utilizing religious dogma.

Dietrich Bonhoeffer saw that this forced adolescence was keeping the Church in a state of complacency and allowing for the critics to continue to reject and render useless the gospel of Jesus Christ. Pastor Bonhoeffer proposed the concept of a "religionless Christianity" which has been called by some "secular theology". Religionless Christianity would allow for a responsible Christian Church to usher Christ's presence into the world around us ("etsi dues non daretur"- as if God was not there).

"God lets Himself be pushed out of the world on to the cross. He is weak and powerless in the world, and that is precisely the way, the only way, in which

He is with us and helps us. Matthew chapter 8 verse 17 makes it quite clear that Christ helps us, not by virtue of his omnipotence, but by virtue of His weakness and suffering".- Dietrich Bonhoeffer

Dietrich Bonhoeffer took his theology (understanding of God) serious and allowed that to guide his conscience. Looking at the world through his view of how God works and what God would have a Christian do, Dietrich Bonhoeffer truly lived out the words he once wrote "When Christ calls a man, he bids him come and die". The astonishing fact is that Dietrich Bonhoeffer was offered the opportunity to leave the crisis in Germany and teach at a school in New York City, yet when he examined himself he wrote:

"I must live through this difficult period in our national history with the people of Germany. I will have no right to participate in the reconstruction of Christian life in Germany after the war if I do not share the trials of this time with my people".

Five weeks after being in New York, Dietrich Bonhoeffer returned to Germany, to stand against the ills of the Third Reich. Bonhoeffer dared to oppose Hitler's regime and reform the apathetic state church by speaking out, establishing an underground seminary, and truly becoming a "man for others". With his last words being, "This is the end, for me the beginning of life", Dietrich Bonhoeffer was hung by the Nazi's as a martyr of the Christian faith on April 9, 1945.

"The Church is the Church only when it exists for others...the Church must share in the secular problems of ordinary human life, not dominating, but helping and serving. I must tell men of every calling, what it means to live in Christ, to exist for others".

- Dietrich Bonhoeffer

Richard Wurmbrand lived a life that clearly demonstrated the truth of how Christians are called to take a stance and deal with the issues around us, whether we live or die. In his book, Tortured for Christ, Richard Wurmbrand tells his story of when the Communists came to power in Russia beginning August 23, 1944. Utilizing discernment and courage, Richard Wurmbrand stood against the seduction the Communists use to control the Church:

"The Communists convened a congress of all Christian bodies in our Parliament building. There were four thousand priests, pastors, and ministers of all denominations- and these men of God chose Joseph Stalin as honorary president of this congress. At the same time he was president of the World Movement of the Godless and a mass murderer of Christians. One after another, bishops and pastors arose and declared that communism and Christianity are fundamentally the same and could coexist. One minister after another said words of praise toward communism and assured the new government of the loyalty of the Church. My wife and I were present at this congress. Sabina told me, "Richard, stand up and wash away this shame from the face of Christ! They are spitting in His face". I said to her, "If I do so, you lose your husband".

She replied, "I don't wish to have a coward as a husband". Then I arose and spoke to this congress, praising not the murderers of Christians, but Jesus Christ, stating that our loyalty is due first to Him. The speeches at this congress were broadcast and the whole country could hear proclaimed from the rostrum of the Communist Parliament the message of Christ! Afterward I had to pay for this, but it was worthwhile"- Excerpt from Tortured for Christ

I felt compelled to share that entire passage because I cannot read that without feeling a stir of zeal within me. Oh, how I long to be summoned to stand for Christ like that. The question is important, would we be willing to stand up and speak out against those "spitting in the face of Jesus" and be willing to die, or would we be cowards and allow the disgrace to continue? Richard Wurmbrand eventually served 14 years being tortured within the Communist prison, and his wife, Sabina, served 3 years in a Communist work camp. The courageous zeal of Richard Wurmbrand led to the formation of the underground Church in Russia and eventually the non-profit, inter-denominational organization, dedicated to aiding and assisting the persecuted Church worldwide; The Voice of the Martyrs.

The courage to stand for Christ comes in many forms and whether it's a stance for truth, a stance for the love and welfare of other people, or a stance against "spitting in the face of Jesus Christ", all of these stem from the call of Christ for us to die to ourselves and truly be missional people. Agnes Gonxha Bojaxhiu, today known and remembered as Mother Teresa of Calcutta, heard a "call within a call" to go and live among and serve the poorest of the poor in Calcutta.

At the age of 12, Mother Teresa felt the call of God on her life to be a missionary of God's love, and by 18 years of age, she joined the Sisters of Our Lady of Loreto, an Irish community of nuns. I love reading about Mother Teresa, because her love for the Lord and humility are so apparent, yet throughout her diaries she is honest in regards to feeling loneliness, despair, and doubt at many times. I have always heard people refer to Mother Teresa, but I was filled with a "holy envy" when I read Shane Claiborne's account of spending the summer visiting and serving with her in his book, The Irresistible Revolution. In his book, he makes clear the death to self and missional love that Mother Teresa embodied as she lived for the glory of Jesus Christ, especially in the following story:

"Mother Teresa was one of those people who sacrificed great privilege because she encountered such great need. People often ask me what Mother Teresa was like. Sometimes it's like they wonder if she glowed in the dark or had a halo. She was short, wrinkled, and precious, maybe even a little ornery, like a beautiful, wise old granny. But there is one thing I will never forget- her feet. Her feet were deformed. Each morning in Mass, I would stare at them. I wondered if she had contracted leprosy. But I wasn't going to ask, of course. "Hey Mother what's wrong with your feet?" One day a sister said to us, "Have you noticed her feet?" We nodded curious. She said, "Her feet are deformed because we get just enough donated shoes for everyone, and Mother does not want anyone to get stuck with the worst pair, so she digs through and finds them. And years of doing that have deformed her feet." Years of loving her neighbor as herself deformed her feet".

Reading that story illustrates to me that most deeds that I claim as "loving my neighbor", do not even come close to intentionally loving my neighbor as myself. I will help people when I am able and if it works for me, but how far would I go to intentionally make myself uncomfortable to enable someone else to have comfort?

I love the challenge, and many times I have and still do long for the opportunity to do so. Mother Teresa had written leaders within the Catholic Church to explain her calling to live among the poorest of the poor and to see Christ in those whom He loves, which illustrates the common Indian greeting Namaste, meaning "I bow to the divinity in you".

"Calcutta's are everywhere if we only have eyes to see. Find your Calcutta"- Mother Teresa

What Biblical truths do you think need to be expounded upon and defended even in the event of disrupting the status quo in Christianity? What oppressed people to you feel the need to stand up for, even in the event you will be persecuted with them? Where do you see the need to wipe the shame away from the face of Jesus Christ? And finally, where and who can you love with a self-sacrificial love?

Imagine what it would look like if we took the challenge to answer the call within a call, as Mother Teresa did, to become the mighty people of God who preach the gospel in word and deed. The call to become "freaked-out" by the Biblical gospel and allow the outpouring to "turn the world upside down".

It simply starts with searching ourselves and finding the things that inspire us and burden us. Think about it. What brings you immense joy when you think, hear, read, or see it? Recognizing your inspiration allows you to build your character, your legacy, and begin to become the change you want to see in the world. In contrast, what bothers you when you think, see, hear, or read it? When you figure out your burdens you have discovered your challenge. Change will start with you, therefore you must begin to fix or abolish the things that bother you- only then will you start a movement, a force to be reckoned with.

Martin Luther tacked his 95 Thesis to the door of the Wittenberg Church in order to initiate reform, yet today the age of information makes book publishing the proper venue, and in line with a zeal empowered by knowledge, I will engage the emerging reformation.

I can account that I will not be complacent or apathetic about the reforms that are needed. Yet it is imperative that others stand with me. As Phyllis Tickle, author and founding editor of the Religion Department of Publishers Weekly noted, every 500 years the Church goes through a rummage sale reform and she calls the one on the horizon The Great Emergence, dare I say an emergency. We have many grumblers in the Church, those that gossip about and criticize the Church for all its problems from decaying theology to dry worship, institutionalized spirituality, judgementalism, and the list goes on. So what do we do? Stop grumbling! Get a hold of your faith in the God we profess, and put your efforts on the Promised Land, in this case the emerging reformation. After all, to poke fun at mathematical prophecy, Martin Luther's reform was in 1517 which gives us until 2017 to fulfill the 500 year rummage reform, although the world might just end in 2012. We must start now!

It is time that we become the body of Christ by means of a reform that will enable us to face what Dietrich Bonhoeffer called the world come of age, or as many call our society today- postmodern. The call to reform is that we live as dead men, dead to ourselves and alive in Christ (Galatians 2:20), therefore we will not act as cowards and have the courage to stand up and wipe the spit away from the Lord Jesus Christ's' face. It is as a body of Believers who are crucified with Christ that Christ will live and we will truly become the answer to all the ills of the world, and as the gospel was intended, to bring healing to the nations (Revelation 22:2).

Answer the call! End your world! Develop an understanding of all that the gospel of Jesus Christ has to offer in your life and the world at large. I continually make the plea for our generation to stop wasting their lives, living with no purpose, chasing things that leave no lasting value.

This way of life has damaging effects of self-hatred, suicide, drug abuse, violence, and worse. What do you, or even we as a culture, have to lose? Jim Elliot, the American missionary who died spreading the gospel, knew this all too well and once stated: "He is no fool who gives what he cannot keep to gain that which he cannot lose".

That's my altar call! Let us begin to see what is on the horizon and truly become the "freaked-out" missionaries who care about nothing more than bringing glory to Jesus Christ. Let us begin to network with one another and lovingly critique all things in need of reform.

It is time that you heed the call, let this book be the cause, and YOU become the sent. As you learn more and more about the gospel of Jesus Christ begin to cry out, act up, preach, live, and get as undignified as possible to spread the kingdom of God. That my fellow Christ-followers is how we will turn the world upside-down in cahoots with the 1st Century Church!

Let the emergence continue and the reformation begin!

> "There remains for us only the very narrow way, often extremely difficult to find, of living every day as though it were our last, and yet living in faith and responsibility as though there were to be a great future." - Dietrich Bonhoeffer

THE EMERGING REFORMATION GET INVOLVED!

The Freaked-Out Movement: C.H.U.R.C.H. is designed to cultivate a collection of radical followers of Christ who desire to bring the healing of the nations through the gospel of Jesus Christ.

Creating
Heartened
Unrelenting
Radical
Christ
Habitués

We believe in the value of conversation, and as we intentionally network with one another, ultimately to bring glory to God, we can do all things through Jesus Christ who strengthens us.

There is no limit to what we envision. The Freaked-Out Movement: C.H.U.R.C.H. simple seeks to answer the call of what is seen on the horizon- the emerging reformation.

The emerging reformation is bringing the gospel of Jesus Christ, the Church, the missionality, and other vital aspects of the "healing of the nations" to new paradigms.

Just imagine . . .

That's your call. Get involved! Let's begin simply conversing and networking to build the kingdom of God on earth as in heaven. Start by sending an email to Pastor Michael Miano (p.mike_miano@yahoo.com).

> **Maybe you** will plant a C.H.U.R.C.H. in your area

> **Maybe you** will become a fellow reformer in leading the Church

> **Maybe you** will be called to do something outrageous for the kingdom of God

BIBLIOGRAPHY

Batterson, M. (2009). Primal: A Quest for the Lost Soul of Christianity. Multnomah Books.

Bell, R. (2006). Velvet Elvis: Repainting the Christian Faith . Zondervan.

Bondar, A. (2010). Reading the Bible through New Covenant Eyes. Baltimore: Publish America.

Bonhoeffer, D. (1966). The Cost of Discipleship. New York: Macmillan.

Bruggerman, W. (2001). The Prophetic Imagination, 2nd Edition. Minneapolos: Augsburg Fortress.

Ca, C. (1968). The Teachings of Don Juan: A Yaqui Way of Knowledge. New York: Washington Square Press.

Chan, F. (2008). Crazy Love: Overwhelmed by a Relentless God. Colorado Springs: David C. Cook.

Claiborne, S. (2006). The Irresistible Revolution: Living as an Ordinary Radical. Grand Rapids: Zondervan.
Claiborne, S., & Haw, C. (2008). Jesus for President: Politics for Ordinary Radicals. Grand Rapids: Zondervan.

Curran, P. R. (N/A). Walking Toward True Hope and Vision. N/A: N/A.

Foster, D. (2006). A Renegade's Guide to God: Finding Life Outside Conventional Christianity. New York: FaithWords.

Hirsch, A. (2006). The Forgotten Ways: Reactivating the Missional Church. Grand Rapids: Brazos Press.

Joyner, R. (2003). The Sword and the Torch. Wilkesboro: Morningstar Publications, Inc.

Kraybill, D. B. (2003). The Upside-Down Kingdom . Scottsdale: Herald Press.

Life Application Study, Publishers., Tyndale House. (1991). Bible: New International Version. Wheaton, Ill.: Zondervan Publishing House.

Rainer, T., & Geiger, E. (2006). Simple Church: Returning to God's Process for Making Disciples. Nashville: B&H Publishing Group.

Talk, D. C. (1999). Jesus Freaks: Stories of Those Who Stood for Jesus : The Ultimate Jesus Freaks. Albury Publishing.

Tickle, P. (2008). The Great Emergence: How Christianity Is Changing and Why. Grand Rapids: Baker Books.

APPENDIX

When I was first introduced to Brother Paul Richard Jr. Curran as a means to get on the list to attend Protestant services at Auburn Correctional Facility, he demonstrated the intentionally missional attitude that should be alive in Christians today. I include this letter to demonstrate the intentional wisdom that Brother Paul used to reach out to a lost young man.

"Brother Mike,

In the name of our Lord and King Yeshua, I pray that all is well with you.

Please excuse my taking the liberty to write to you. My reason for doing so is twofold. The first concerns you, and the second concerns others, through you.

Don't take this the wrong way but since that day "Rock" introduced us, the Lord has laid it on my heart to "train you up". The confirmation of this came when you disclosed that you love history. The gifts I have are as teacher, watchman, eventually apostle, and prophet. The two gifts I am to share with you is teacher and watchman. The other two only the Lord can train you for and it all depends on your relationship with Him.

There are two types of teachers. There are evangelistic teachers, and prophetic teachers. The evangelistic teacher focuses on salvation, which is also called seed planting and foundation laying. The prophetic teacher focuses on teaching how to see our world (economically, politically, historically, socially, etc...) through the eyes and ears of the Word. This type of teaching is also referred to as watering, meat distribution, etc . . . Oh evangelistic teachers also teach the milk of the Word; basic doctrine. Both of these two types of teaching is illustrated in 1 Corinthians chapter 3. The prophetic teacher must learn how to depend on the Holy Ghost for wisdom. I already see that you are open to the Holy Ghost because you get excited over revelation.

There are two stages to wisdom which a prophetic teacher a watchman must encounter. The first is the fear of the Lord (see, Psalm 111:10, Proverbs 1:7 & 9:10). The second stage is understanding (see, Proverbs 4: 5-7, 10:23, Matthew 13:23). It is possible to believe without understanding, and there is a difference between having faith, believing, and having hope. They are not the same. I wrote a small book about this difference, and when I get it back I will let you read it. Anyway, understanding is the water which is sprinkled on the seed (see, Proverbs 16:22). As you read in 1 Corinthians chapter 2, there are two sources from where wisdom (understanding) can come from; man (carnal) or Holy Ghost (spiritual). For the most part, the Church is walking by mans' wisdom. I will get more into this depending on your response to this.

If you read Ezekiel chapter 33, you will see the office of a watchman told of. One thing you must remember in these two gifts (prophetic teacher and watchman)

"Let God be true and every man a liar (Romans 3:4)". Jesus is the Word (John 1:14), Jesus is the Truth (John 4:23-24, 14:6), and no lie is of the truth (1 John 2:21). Jesus told us to try the trees by their fruits (Matthew 7:15-20) and He told us what this fruit we are supposed to try is in Matthew 12:33-37. Once you are properly equipped you will have awesome sight, and you will challenge "pastors, reverends, etc.". If any person speaks against the Word, by teaching false understanding (bitter water, see James 3:8-13) we are to correct it.

But, this office is a lonely one because we are told that the day would come when His people, and people in general, will not endure sound doctrine, but will rather love lies (2 Timothy 4:3-4). We are not out to please people though (see, Matthew 10:22-40 and Galatians 1:10).

Being that I am led to distribute my talents to you, it does not mean I expect you to follow me, hang out with me all the time, etc...It will require you to make time for us to study together, and I have a lot of stuff written already, so it will all be up to you.

Our studying must begin in the Old Testament because to walk in the offices I am to equip you for, you must have a good understanding of what happened in Israel. Most of what is taught today is false. Then we will get into the books of the prophets also.

You will learn how the first three beasts of Daniel chapter 7 come together to form the first Revelation 13 beast, who these beasts of Daniel chapter 7 are, and how the first Revelation 13 beast, and the fourth beast of Daniel 7 is the fourth kingdom of Daniel chapter 2. This all correlates with Ezekiel chapter 17 also. I am confident that you will pick it up fairly easy, and revelation will spur you to study more; especially when you see how all of this pertains to history and politics.

Now for the second reason I write this. Again, please don't take this the wrong way. When you write to your mom again, could you ask her if she has anyone out there who will correspond with me so that I can teach out there too? I'd like to write a letter to your mom, which you will send, and if you want you can, read it too, so that I can show your mom that I am not after money, packages, etc...My priority is ministry, and if the Lords' will is that I make a few friends along the way, great . . . (Portion deleted, personal) . . . As soon as I am able, I am going to invest in getting put on a prison pen pal website so that I might obtain ministry opportunities.

If you decide no to the second point, I'll understand, and it doesn't change the first. Again, please don't take either the wrong way. I value our friendship, and I wouldn't do anything to make you look bad, or violate your trust.

Well brother, God bless
You brother and Co-laborer,

Paul

When I met Pastor Alan Bondar and he shared his views concerning eschatology, I thought he was out of his mind. Alan challenged my understandings with Scripture and I went home and began to search the Scriptures.

I ended up emailing him some of my thoughts and he responded. Here I will share our email conversations back and forth.

> **Mike:** I have always read through the prophetic accounts of Matthew chapters 24-25 as being partially fulfilled, and understood the context to be a future account of the end times.

> **Alan:** The accounts of Matthew 24 and 25 are about end times and they were future account from the perspective of the original audience.

> **Mike:** As far as judgment, I have read through the Scriptures to be an actual time of judgment at the second coming of Jesus Christ, when we will all stand before Christ and give an account of our lives and be sent to heaven or hell (2 Corinthians chapter 5).

> **Alan:** Again, the judgment was an actual time of judgment at the 2nd coming of Jesus Christ. And when the Scriptures state "WE will all stand before the judgment seat of Christ", they did all stand before the judgment seat of Christ. At that judgment, all entered into either eternal life or eternal death. Nowhere do the Scriptures state that anyone entered into Heaven at the judgment. That idea is imposed on the text because of the wrong presupposition that the judgment is still future to us. Also, hell is the Greek word, "gehenna". Gehenna was a real place outside our Jerusalem where dead bodies were thrown to be burned.

Because of the nature of the constant fires going in Gehenna, the invisible realm of Hades came to be referred to as hell, or Gehenna. So when Jesus states, "Do not fear him who can destroy the body only, but fear Him who is able to cast both the body and soul in Gehenna", He was playing on the commonly held view that the invisible place was represented by the visible place. He is not teaching that both body and soul go to the invisible place.

Mike: As far as resurrection, I have always read and understood that our souls sleep (1 Thessalonians chapter 4). Then at the coming of Jesus Christ, we will be raised from the dead (1 Corinthians chapter 15), judged, and sent to heaven or hell.

Alan: The problem with soul sleep is that "sleep" is used as a euphemism for death. Scriptures speak of sheol (Hebrew)/ Hades (Greek), an actual place for the dead (Cf. Luke 17). One major problem that futurism has is that until the coming of Christ and the judgment, Hades is still around. And if you look at the judgment text in Matthew chapter 25, you can see that eternal life is given at judgment. So if the judgment has not happened yet, then nobody has eternal life. In addition, if this is true, then we also must still be under the Old Covenant Law. Jesus said in Matthew 5:18:

> "For I truly say to you, until heaven and earth pass away, not the smallest letter or stroke shall pass from the Law until all is accomplished".

If we are still waiting for heaven and earth to pass away, then the Law is still binding. But as it stands, heaven and earth refer to the old mode of existence.

If you do a survey of the Old Testament for "heavens and earth", you'll find that the phrase refers to God's covenant and God's covenant people. God calls Israel "heavens and earth" in Isaiah, for example.

Regarding the resurrection, the dead were raised and given eternal life. Again, nowhere do the Scriptures teach that anyone went to heaven at the resurrection or the judgment. The difficulty in understanding the resurrection is that it is assumed that it has to do with the physical body. It does not. But more on that below.

Mike: The kingdom of God is both a present and future reality. We are told that the kingdom of God is within us, and that the kingdom of God is love, peace, and joy in the Holy Spirit (Romans 14), but also Jesus Christ has told us that we will eat and drink with Him in the kingdom (Luke 22: 29-30).

Alan: Actually, Jesus said this to the apostles, not to us. And they would sit on twelve thrones and judge the twelve tribes. This doesn't sound universal to me. It sounds very covenantal. This is not about literal eating and drinking or sitting on literal thrones judging the literal tribes. This imagery is explained by John in Revelation 21.

Mike: I do agree and believe that the Scriptures were written to a said people at a said time. For instance, the book of Romans was written to the Roman church at that time, and dealt with their situations. We can read in context and get lessons from what it meant to them.

Does it essentially matter if Jesus Christ came back already or we are waiting for Him to come? I have heard arguments on both sides of this discussion, but I believe if we read through the Word in proper context and learn from it, it really doesn't matter all that much.

Alan: Yes. If you think about your question, it really doesn't make any sense to say that we are reading the Word in proper context and then stating that we are still waiting for Jesus to return. Also, as you will come to understand with time, once our learned presuppositions are dropped and we can read the Bible through New Covenant Eyes, there is a lot more wrong with the traditional understanding of things than we might have first thought. A few of those will be exposed below in response to some of your other questions.

But, initially, I will say that if Jesus and the apostles were wrong about the timing of His coming, then how can we trust anything else that they taught? If you ask somebody to whom you are evangelizing to read Matthew 15:27-28, and ask them to tell you what it says, they would say, "It says Jesus would come in the glory of His father with His angels before all of the people He was talking to died". They would come to that conclusion because that's what it says.

But if you were to say to them in response, "Jesus didn't come in the glory of His Father with His angels yet" then on what grounds would you have to say to them that any other text, such as Romans 6:23 means what it says. You see, in my opinion, I think the doctrine of the second coming of Christ is the primary reason why relativism has grown so strong over time. The church has unwittingly set the tone for it. Try telling someone that you aren't a relativist after reading Matthew 16:27-28 and saying that Jesus hasn't come yet. Frankly, I'm amazed that anyone comes to Christ when we don't even believe the very Scriptures we teach from. Evangelism is far more effective when we show people that we believe what the Scriptures say.

Mike: What is salvation?

Alan: Salvation is what you always thought it was. We deserve eternal death, but in Christ, we have eternal life. At biological death, believers go to heaven; unbelievers go to the place of the eternally dead.

Mike: Eternal age of grace (world will never end?) What about situations like 2012, etc. . . ?

Alan: Situations like 2012? Are the end of the world scenarios rooted in Scripture or hype?

Mike: What exactly happened in 70 AD?

Alan: Jerusalem was destroyed. The Old Covenant was brought to and end by the destruction of the Temple. The New Covenant was consummated. The coming, the resurrection, and the judgment occurred. The marriage of Christ to the bride was consummated. The age to come began and so did eternal life and eternal death.

Mike: What is evangelism from the preterist view? Why?

Alan: Evangelism is sharing the Gospel that the Messiah is King and had died and rose for our sins, fulfilled the law on our behalf so that we could have eternal life. If you believe this, than you have eternal life. Why evangelize?

Because unless we share the Gospel, how does anyone know the Gospel in order to believe it?

Mike: What is heaven / hell?

Alan: Heaven is where believers go after biological death. Hell (Gehenna) was the part of Hades that the wicked went to after biological death. Hades has been swallowed up by eternal death. Now there is Heaven, and the place of the eternally dead (to my knowledge, Scripture does not give us the name of this place). The lake of fire is the status of the non-elect. It is used only figuratively as imagery in the Scriptures. We have become accustomed to calling the place the unbeliever goes to after death as the lake of fire. And I am alright with that. So I call it the lake of fire, although that may not technically be correct since the Scriptures don't actually call the place the lake of fire.

Mike: Why has this understanding been lost so long?

Alan: Snowball effect. I actually deal with this question pretty extensively in my book. Believe it or not, there was some tampering of the Scriptures that occurred in the second century to fit the postponement theory of the coming of Christ. There is actually evidence of this that I put forth in my book. At any rate, the point being, once the copies of the Scriptures containing this tampering got into everyone's hands, even now that we have the originals, it's really hard to get people to consider that the Church just might have been wrong. Plus, if you think about it, it shouldn't be all that inconceivable that this understanding has been lost for so long. How long did it take the Church to develop the doctrine of the Trinity? Or the Incarnation? Or Faith alone? If the church took 15 hundred years to develop some of these doctrines, then it is very likely that they got this wrong, especially when you consider the fact that eschatology was never the focus of any council throughout history. And I believe there is so much that needs to be developed. We haven't even scratched the surface.

Mike: Why the book of Revelation?

Alan: I'm not sure I understand this question. But I'll stab at it. Revelation was written to communicate to the first century audience the end was about to happen in conjunction with the destruction of Jerusalem. That's what the whole book is about. Compare the language in Revelation with Isaiah 13, which is a prophecy about the destruction of Babylon occurring 15 years after Isaiah 13 was written.

Mike: Preterist? Hyper, partial, etc. . . ?

Alan: Preterism means past fulfillment. Full preterists believe that all prophecy was fulfilled. Partial preterists believe that 70 AD fulfilled some of the prophecies, but not the 2nd coming, judgment, or resurrection. Partial preterists believe that Matthew 24 was fulfilled in 70 AD because of the time texts and the direct reference to the Temple buildings, but Matthew 25 is still future. The problem I have with that view is that it is completely rooted in presupposition. There is no indication in the text that Matthew 25 is about anything different than Matthew 24. Plus, in both Matthew 24:30-31 and Matthew 25:31 it is stated that Jesus would come in glory with angels. How partial preterists arrive at the conclusion that one of them is invisible and one of them is visible is beyond me.

Mike: Reading from The Allurement of Hymenaen Preterism by Jim West, the purpose of Christ's resurrection was to justify the whole man- body and soul (Romans 8:23). "If Hymanaeus meant that the bodily resurrection of the believer is already past, he would have been speaking nonsense, for he himself would have bodily resurrected".

Alan: This is an argument from a futurist who misunderstands the bodily resurrection. Preterists believe in the bodily resurrection, but we do not mean the biological body. Go to newcovenanteyes.ning and read my article on the resurrection of the body.

Mike: A low view of the body - Gnostics felt all flesh was evil and Greeks "body is the prison of the soul" (Plato). Didn't early Christianity and even Paul dispute that?

Alan: Yes. Full preterists do not believe that the body is the prison of the soul. Ironically, it's the futurist position that ends up with the Gnostic view. If you think about it, futurists maintain that the biological body is still evil, and that's why it has to die. So in futurism, the soul is righteous but the body is evil. That's the whole spirit is good and matter is evil heresy of Gnosticism. Either way you spin it, that's what futurism teaches.

Mike: Matthew 24: "that day" (Matthew 7:21-23; Acts 17:31). I cannot understand how this would be viewed as a universal day of judgment, physical not Spiritual, and how it could have happened in 70 AD? Even consider chapter 25 verse 2.

Alan: I assume you meant 25:32? Here is the interesting thing about that: Compare the first part of chapter 25 with the second part of chapter 25. Jesus spoke using parabolic language and never clarified that He switched to literal language. It is our presupposition of a physical judgment that forces the change. Nothing in the text remotely implies a change. Regarding "that day", is this a different "that day" than the day of the Parousia? If there is not only one "that day", then who's to say that there aren't 5 comings of Jesus? Why stop at 2?

Mike: "The Hymaneans repeatedly fail to distinguish between the last days of Israel, and the last day at the end of the world".

Alan: Where does the Bible teach about the end of the world? This is a presupposed, non-Biblical idea. Paul's response to the Hymanean heresy actually demonstrates that full preterism must be true. But rather than looking at the argument that Paul makes, futurists hone in on the fact that Hymaneaus said that the resurrection already happened and claim that full preterists have the same heresy. Here is my understanding of Paul's response to their heresy:

1.) Hymaneaus and Philetus claimed that Christ had already come while the Temple was still standing. It is no secret that the Judaizers continued to cause trouble in the churches during the time the apostles were writing. This is why there is a plethora of teaching concerning circumcision and dietary and sundry laws. Paul was teaching a law-free Gospel, but Judaizers insisted that Christ was insufficient. They insisted that the Law of the Old Covenant system still had to be kept to inherit salvation.

2.) Thus, the heresy of Hymaneaus and Philetus was directly related to the Old Covenant system still being in effect. In other words, they were teaching that the Old Covenant system had equal authority with Christ.

The reason that their heresy was able to upset the faith of some was because if the resurrection had already happened while the Temple remained standing, then Paul was wrong- the Gospel isn't Law-free.

3.) Paul quotes from Numbers 16 dealing with the issue of authority to correct the heresy. Quoting Preston:

> "The issue in Numbers was one of authority, a question of identity (Numbers 16:3-5). Was Moses to be the sole leader, or would others share in that authority? The issue in Timothy was, "Nevertheless...the Lord knows who are His (2 Timothy 2:19). It is a question of identity".

If authority wasn't the issue at stake in 2 Timothy 2, then why would Paul quote from Numbers 16 in response to the heresy? Most interpreters ignore the fact that Paul is quoting from Numbers 16. But the issue of authority is in fact what Paul has in mind, and that is made clear by the context of this quote.

4.) The heresy was specifically tied to when the coming would happen. For Hymaneaus and Philetus, the Old Covenant system had equal authority with Christ. For Paul, the coming of Christ would be the very thing that would destroy the Old Covenant system which was vying for authority.

The reason Hymaneaus and Philetus were able to overthrow the faith of some is because, according to them, Christ came and the Temple was still standing. Paul's response in essence, "Christ doesn't share His authority. When He comes, the Temple won't be standing".

5.) Thus, Paul's use of Numbers 16 demonstrates that when the Temple would fall, it is at that time that Christ would have come. The Temple was intimately tied to the Old Covenant. Hymaneaus and Philetis understood that as long as the Temple was standing, the Old Covenant still had authority. The people who had their faith upset understood that as well. And Paul most definitely understood that.

His response to the heresy implicitly demonstrates the reason that coming of Christ hadn't yet happened was because the Temple was still standing.

And his use of Numbers 16 requires that the true authority would demonstrate Himself through the destruction of the Temple. What will have occurred once the true authority had demonstrated Himself? The resurrection.

6.) The way Paul corrects the heresy of Hymaneus and Philetus requires that full preterism must be true- that is, unless the Old Covenant system is still in effect, and that, without a Temple.

Mike: 1 Thessalonians 4-16- Paul's purpose is to impart comfort to the living about the dead (this is why he numbers himself with the living), to prophesy that his generation would escape death all together.

Alan: Actually, that's not exactly true. Paul expected that some in his generation would be alive at the coming of Christ. In verse 17, Paul says, "Then WE who are alive and remain…”. If audience relevancy matters, than Paul is talking about people alive in the first century.

Mike: What about the empty tomb? Jesus' resurrection must have been, and was bodily (People seen Him, Thomas was commanded to touch Him, He ate with them).

Alan: That is correct. Nobody is contending that.

Mike: In reading from A Brief Theological Analysis of Hyper-Preterism by Kenneth Gentry, "If all the prophecy was fulfilled in the 1st century events, then who is to say that it is the will of God for the gospel to exercise worldwide victory?

Alan: Here is my question: Do the Scriptures teach worldwide victory post 70 AD? Paul stated that the Gospel did go to the whole world, and to all the nations. That prophecy was fulfilled according to Paul. The problem with Gentry's question is that it makes the spread of the Gospel today prophetic instead of principal.

I have no problem with spreading the Gospel because the Gospel continues to bring healing to the nations. But I do have a problem with saying that we are still fulfilling prophecy that the Gospel will spread to the whole world before the end will come when Paul already said that happened.

Mike: Consider this statement concerning creedal failure: "First, hyper-preterism is heterodox. It is outside the creedal orthodoxy of Christianity. No creed allows any second advent in AD 70. No creed allows any other type of resurrection than a bodily one. Historic creeds speak of the universal, personal judgment of all men, not of a representative judgment in A.D. 70.

It would be most remarkable if the entire Church that came through A.D. 70 missed the proper understanding of the eschaton and did not realize its members had been resurrected! And that the next generations had no inkling of the great transformation that took place! Has the entire Christian Church missed the basic contours of Christian eschatology for its first 1900 years?"

Alan: So what? Do we determine truth by creeds or by Scripture? The problem with this whole statement is that it is rooted in the presupposition that bodily resurrection is biological. Full preterists do not deny a bodily resurrection. And since it isn't biological, then it is not that inconceivable that the entire church did not realize that its members had been resurrected. They were looking for a biological resurrection.

Mike: What about those that lived in or around 70 AD? Clement of Rome, Jude's grandsons, also consider the Didache. Why not mention of this 2nd coming?

Alan: Again, this presents no problem to preterism. This argument is based on the idea that people like Clement and Jude's grandsons must have understood this stuff because they were there and were taught by the Apostles. But if that's true, then why do we even have the New Testament?

In other words, aren't the letters in the New Testament written to deal with problems of understanding within the first century church? Weren't they all taught by the Apostles? Then how did they misunderstand so many things? How did the Apostles, whom Jesus taught, mess things up so many times?

Mike: Do preterists believe we are in our resurrected state, currently?

Alan: Yes.

Mike: Adam's sin had physical effects on the world-consider Genesis chapter 3. Will any of this ever end? How, why, or why not?

Alan: The idea that Adam's sin had physical effects on the world is eisegeted into Genesis 3. The text doesn't teach that.

Mike: Consider the Greek view of the resurrection, preterism sounds pretty similar. But Paul in Athens seemed to show something different and also expressed that he agreed with the Pharisee view of the resurrection (Acts 23:6-9; 24:15, 21; Revelation 20).
Alan: The Greek view of the resurrection is platonic. Full preterism doesn't teach that at all. We're arguing for a complete change/resurrection of the same body. It has nothing to do with biology. Paul agreed with the Pharisees that there would be a resurrection of the dead. Nowhere does Paul state that he agreed with their view of what that meant. But there was most certainly a resurrection of the dead. We today, who are in Christ, are not dead. So we don't need to be resurrected. Jesus said that whoever believes in Me will live. And whoever lives will never die.

Mike: Did Jesus Christ physically return in 70 AD?

Alan: No. And nowhere did He state that He would.

What He did say was that He would come again in the glory of His Father. His Father is not physical. But He is invisible. So for Christ to come in the glory of His Father would require that it be non-physical and non-visible.

Mike: I have a hard time accepting that God would allow the world to continue forever. How could God continue this sinful world forever? Were the promises a lie? There is no final conclusion to mans' rebellion?

Alan: This is based on the assumption that the presence of sin is a bad thing. Apart from sin, what would drive us to God when we cannot fully see His glory? Plus, the beauty of this sinful world continuing forever is that there is no end to the inclusion of people into His kingdom. There was a final conclusion to mans' rebellion- Christ. That's what the gospel is all about. In Christ we find the end to mans' rebellion. He is our righteousness.

Mike: "The full failure of the first Adam must be overcome by the full success of the Second Adam".

Alan: That is correct. And it was.

Mike: Also, is God still with us (until the end)?

Alan: There is no other end then the end of the Old Covenant. So God is still with us forever. The New Covenant has no end.

Mike: Were all nations, just the surrounding nations, therefore it was only them that received judgment?

Alan: That is correct. Nations can only be defined by the context. When God told David that all nations would fear him, was He speaking of nations that exist today? How many nations do you know that fear David? Based on what grounds would we determine that Jesus is speaking of nations beyond the ones in His generation?

Mike: What about the Lord's Supper (1 Corinthians 11:26)?

Alan: The Lord's Supper ceased at the Parousia of Christ and His marriage to His bride. The whole point of the Lord's Supper was to participate in His death while the Groom was away until the Groom would return and they would all be resurrected.

I AM FREE TO LOVE
a blog post on September 10, 2010

Well friends, today or rather yesterday I completed my 30 days of reading through the Bible (this was supposed to be in a Ramadan fashion, but safe to admit I didn't fast properly and didn't get to attend any iftar's with Muslims, not exactly happy about that, but life goes on).

Anyways, reading through the Word of God is always a journey and new truths speak out every time, this time even more than any other time. Honestly, these last couple weeks I feel like I have been getting a handle on this whole "Good News" thing. Truthfully, when I ask many (not all) other Christians what the "good news" is that we call "gospel", I don't understand what they see as good news, and I don't think they see it either.

So, really what is the "good news" that Christ came to tell us? Well let's look back. We know that God instituted the Old Covenant with the Israelite people in order to draw a people unto Himself, who would give Him glory and could have a sample of His presence by following the Law.

Only through sacrifice and obedience could God be sought out. Just think of life like that, "touch not, taste not", as we read about the Ark of the Covenant and all these religious themes we can sense the fear the people had of being "cursed by God". The really radical thing that we continually see is that God has always wanted the deeper things such as the heart and love of man rather than simple outward religious faith.

I Samuel 15:22- "Does the Lord delight in burnt offerings and sacrifices as much as in obeying the voice of the Lord? To obey is better than sacrifice and to heed is better than the fat of the rams".

I would rather advise you to read the entire chapter of Psalms 51, but I will quote a part of it to illustrate my point. "O Lord open my lips, and my mouth will declare your praise. You do not delight in sacrifice, or I would bring it, you do not pleasure in burnt offerings, the sacrifices of God are a broken spirit; a broken and contrite heart (Psalms 51:15-17a)". For more verses read Hosea and Micah.

Do you see it? God does not want the outward stuff, but rather what comes from inside our hearts, and we see Jesus compellingly criticizing the Pharisees of His day concerning these matters. But the Law of the Old Covenant made the outward things necessary!

So then comes this Messiah, the anointed one, who will essentially make "all things new", thus the term "New Covenant". The kingdom (presence) of God and righteousness will no longer need to be a thing sought by men by standards and Law, but rather will "dwell among them". This was a big deal to the 1st Century peoples, especially the religious people. The law of God, or rather the Law of Christ would be written on the hearts of men (Jeremiah 31:33-34, Hebrews 8:6-13 and 10:14-18). What is this law? The law of Christ (1 Corinthians 9:21, Galatians 6:2, amongst other verses that illustrate this point).

So as the title of this blog says, "I am free to love!". Come on sing it, you know the song! What exactly does that mean? I am free from having to tell people they are sinners and must live right because by love I can show them the love of Christ and be a light in the midst of darkness. I am free from having to live a partially sanitized life, but rather can serve God through a life of love and service. I am free to live, to truly be in the world not of it, and I mean really live without stressing "is this a sin", "should I be around these people", "should I be in church right now", etc. That my friends, in the glory of the New Covenant that stressed out the religious people in Jesus' day and continues to do so in religious circles today. Consider the Galatians factor. The church in Galatia had this exact problem, when the religious Jews began to mix with the Gentiles. This religious spirit is clearly called what it is, hypocrisy, because it is against the freedom to love of the Law of Christ. Read Galatians chapter 2:11-21.

> "The only thing that counts is faith expressing itself
> through love." (Galatians 5:6)

Consider the fact that under the Old Covenant Law, even the supposedly righteous religious leader's committed sins against the rules, but yet their outward appearance of being holy, gave them a false sense of righteousness ("I'm better than you"), but it was exactly that FALSE! Christ brought the reality of the Law which was recognizing that even though we are sinners, through love (Christ's law) we can seek His kingdom and His righteousness.

Truly understanding this new, alternative, radical, revolutionary change that Jesus Christ brought into effect is what makes a believer "freak out". Jesus Christ presented the Jews of His time and us today with a new opportunity to experience God. Consider the recent religious cliché' of "It's not about religion, but relationship". Very true!

> "But thanks be to Gold, who always leads us through
> triumphal procession in Christ and through us spreads

everywhere the fragrance of the knowledge of Him. For we are to God the aroma of Christ among those who are being saved and those who are perishing." (2 Corinthians 2:14-15)

I urge you my fellow believers, seek to truly live and read the Word of God through New Covenant Eyes (for more info, check out **newcovenanteyes**.com)

All for the sake of righteousness, peace, and joy,

Mike Miano

WHAT ARE YOU SCREAMING WITH YOUR LIFE? AN ALTERNATIVE STORY

blog post on November 2, 2010

"He set another parable before them, saying, "The Kingdom of Heaven is like a grain of mustard seed, which a man took, and sowed in his field; which indeed is smaller than all seeds. But when it is grown, it is greater than the herbs, and becomes a tree, so that the birds of the air come and lodge in its branches." (Matthew 13:31-32)

Ok, well wanted to make a video because I believe I can explain the passion of the kingdom of God that is welled up inside me so much better on video or in person, but I'm going to try this method.

Lately I realized through reading and talking with others that the Biblical narrative as a story causes some questions.

For example, why did God choose to operate the way He did? Why Jesus? Why the "Kingdom of God, etc. . . I have come to realize there is great reward in understanding the "Kingdom of God", and I'm not talking about some "die and go to heaven stuff", I mean more for the here and now, you know "live your best life now" type of stuff.

So what is it?

Let's take it from the beginning. As you open the book of Genesis you meet Adam and Eve, these are the people who God is in covenant with (which means relationship). Most of us have heard the story of the apple of sin many times, so we know that Adam and Eve disobeyed God. Now God created us for a relationship with Him, so God obviously sees the need for some rules in His people. Now we pause . . .

Why did God want a people?

God in His divine wisdom created the natural order of things, the why's and what's of the world, therefore the reality that all good things start as small movements actually isn't man made sociology (read Margaret Mead) but rather wisdom of God

> "Never doubt that a small group of thoughtful, committed citizens can change the world. Indeed, it is the only thing that ever has" - Margaret Mead

So, God takes this small people come to be known as Israelites (the people of God) and institutes a Law (a fence you could say) to keep them separate from the world.

These are the people God cultivates and blesses through time. Many "prophets" pop up here and there and are a bit radical, some see visions concerning the future that will grow beyond the fence and dream of this (the hope of Israel).

As with any spoiled child, these people of God began to feel self-righteous about there doings, and began to condemn all things that were not as they saw fit, and as time progressed they became divisive and hard hearted to the things of God, it was no longer about God's glory, it became about the preservation of their way of doing things (Biblical language-

Pharisee). Then the Messiah was born. We read about this miraculous virgin birth in the beginning of the biographical books of the Bible (Matthew, Mark, Luke, and John- called they Gospels, which we will get into in a moment).

Jesus Christ, known as the son of Joseph, was born the son of God, to fulfill the hope of Israel- the kingdom of God. This kingdom would be the fulfillment of all that the prophets had spoken about and would be the hope of Israel, this is the good news.

Jesus Christ steps on the scene and immediately declares "The kingdom of God is at hand". Basically the time is now, and he begins to explain.

Now, remember the verse in the beginning of this blog? Re-read it. You see how God works? He started small, instituted a way for this plant to grow separate from weeds and other plants- now he is going to open the gate and let the plant grow in the garden and take over!

Think. Reaping the garden will occur (judgment), cleansing, and then freedom!

As a Christian, you, I and others are this over grown radical garden. The good news Jesus Christ was declaring is that "another world is possible"! He said that to those Jews in His time to let them know the way God has been operating with you guys in the fence is over and a new way is going, and that same concept must be reverberated throughout our time today!

Out of the 12 men that followed Jesus Christ, 11 of them understood what He was saying and drew inspiration from their heroes (the Old Testament Prophets) and as Scripture says "turned the world upside-down".

That is how this kingdom stuff works- we must begin to renew, re-invent, and re-imagine another world!

So my question to you? What exactly are you screaming with your life? How are you growing outside the fence?

Good Inspiration concerning this kingdom:

"We are convinced that Jesus came not to prepare us to die but to teach us how to live. The kingdom of God is not just something we hope for when we die but something we "live on earth as it is in heaven."

" . . . but throughout ages, beautiful saints have lived faithfully, giving us hope that a set part people can fascinate and bless the world."

" . . . a movement of people who stepped out of the empire that was oppressing them and began creating a new way of life."

" . . . Christians should be troublemakers, creators of uncertainty, agents of a dimension incompatible with society."

- Quotes from books written by Shane Claiborne

EMBRACE YOUR VULNERABILITIES ACCESSING THE POWER OF CHRIST

Written by Paul Richard Jr. Curran

The word vulnerable means capable of being wounded: susceptible to wounds, and open to attack. With that said, the reader may ask how our vulnerabilities can help us to access the power of Christ. Some may even say that the title of this writing sounds foolish. The reason for these potential reactions is understood.

Today, by society's standards, we are taught that we are supposed to hide our vulnerabilities until we can trust one another enough to be vulnerable with them.

To me, and to those who are spiritually minded, that reasoning is foolish because we can never know if we can trust someone with our vulnerabilities until we allow ourselves to be vulnerable. This is especially true when it comes to our relationships with others. Another consideration comes into play in relationships.

After we have come to value another in our lives, we tend to hide certain things about ourselves for fear that the other will not accept the new revelation about ourselves; thus they will no longer want to be in our lives. What are some of our vulnerabilities? Our desires, passions, thoughts, sexual and romantic appetites, fantasies, et al. . . . Also our hunger and need to love and to be loved. These and many other of the intangible aspects of who we are compromise our personality.

Personality is defined as a collection of emotional, mental, and behavioral traits that characterize a person. In most cases today, another's true personality is only known to the individual because most have the tendency to emit a personality that is most likely to be accepted by others. What appears to be, and what is, are not necessarily the same. Thus, over time, when a person's true personality comes to the surface, we assume that another is changing. They are not changing.

The change occurred in order to gain acceptance. The only way that we can truly know another's personality is if they allow us into their hearts and minds. Though in a society that tends to shelter itself from their environment, we experience life through illusion, not that which is true.

Most today consider wearing ones heart on their sleeve to be abnormal, eccentric, and even crazy, while the opposite is considered normal. When we live life wearing our hearts on our sleeves, we protect others and ourselves; because all will know who they are dealing with.

The most vulnerable person who ever lived was Christ, and as Christians we are suppose to be as our Master.

When we base our judgments on appearances, which is to walk by sight and operate with a carnal mind, we live contrary to Christ. Also, as will be shown in this article, we live contrary to the will of God in our lives. God does not think as we think, and His ways are not our ways. Whose thoughts and ways are better; Gods' or mans?

If you answered Gods' then let me impart some of Gods' wisdom and truth to you. It is promised that if you incorporate these things in your life, you will experience that life, and life more abundantly, which the Word promises. In order to understand what is and what we are to look for, we must understand what was. Therefore, we will take a trip back to the Garden of Eden.

As Paul instructs, the invisible things of God from the creation of the world are clearly seen, being understood by the things that are made. (See, Romans 1:20) One of the first things we learn about Gods' intent, in creating man, is that He created them to be naked. There mere mention of the word naked may have caused many of you to conjure up images of bodies; some of you may have experienced a tinge of guilt, shame, fear, while others may have all of a sudden felt vulnerable.

If you thought of bodies, you have no clue what nakedness is. If you felt guilt, shame, fear, or vulnerability, you are deceived by your carnal mind. God created each and every one of us to be naked, and He called this nakedness good. Then why do any of us feel guilt, shame, fear toward that which God intended and called good. Why do we equate nakedness to least intimate aspect of our being naked, i.e., physically? The answer is found in the Word of God. Not only did God create man to be naked, He also created them not to have shame, guilt, and fear in regard to their nakedness. This Gods' original intent was for man to be fully vulnerable toward another. Paul tells us to speak the truth to each other in love, confess our faults to each other, etc... When we refuse to do this, for whatever reason we call logical and reasonable, we are acting contrary to love, and are instead living in fear (See, I John 4:11-21).

Some may say that Adam and Eve were not ashamed because they were husband and wife. This is wrong, and is based on

157

the presumption that God created only one man and one woman. After the "fall" of man, we are told that the children of Adam went and took wives, and had children. Where did these other women come from? The Hebrew word for Adam means the individual man, but also means mankind, male and female. Like in every other part of the Bible, we are not told of everything that happened. Jesus talked of other disciples, who were not of the twelve or of those that walked physically with Jesus: yet we know they were there. We are told of the Israelites in the world of the Old Testament, but they were not the only people on the earth; and they didn't even know everyone on the earth.

Likewise, the Bible only talks about Adam and Eve, but this does not mean that they were the only two individuals that God created. Thus, Adam and Eve were not ashamed to be naked in front of anyone. The nakedness which Adam, Eve, and the others who were in the earth, experienced was to wholly delight in, and express, the personalities that God created them to be. This was Gods' intent when He created man is His own image.

The word image does not mean that which can be seen or touched in the physical world. What is seen and touched in the physical world is the manifestation of the image. The image itself remains an idea and a concept. When an architect sits to design a house, the house is conceptualized in their mind first. They create the image of the house, long before anyone else views the manifestation of the house. The same is true concerning Gods' creation of the world, and mankind. God had, and has, a totally unique idea and concept for each and every man and woman alive today. Even our bodies are created according to Gods' image for what He wanted us to look like; and to manifest His image; He caused our parents to be paired up in order to create the image He had. There is nothing that God did not create about us, and He called everything he created good.

Man is born into sin because man is naturally inclined to live contrary to His image. Though, this was not Gods' intent, rather mans choice. How many times do you suppose that Adam and Eve walked by the Tree of Knowledge? Only God knows. Though one day, Satan caused Eve to see this tree in a different light. The first interaction that we are told of, between Eve and Satan was Satan asking Eve a question concerning the only law which God told Adam. Adam, not Eve, was told that they could not eat of the Tree of Knowledge. Somehow, someway, Adam failed his wife because when she was asked the question, she twisted the Word of God by saying that they could not eat of, or touch, the Tree of Knowledge (See, Genesis 2: 16-17; 3:3).

This was all the door that Satan needed to come in. As soon as Eve opened this door, Satan no longer questioned, but rather made statements of conviction to get her to see the tree differently. Now, the tree and its fruit appeared to be good for food, pleasing to the eyes, and sounded like a good thing in order to make one wise. Satan got Eve to think that maybe God withheld something from them, or cheated them of something. After Eve and Adam ate the fruit, they died. They lost touch with who God created them to be.

The result of the Tree of Knowledge, which is wisdom according to carnal standards, will always produce fear, guilt, shame, and insecurity for what a person thinks, feels, desires, and how they look. We, as Adam and Eve, had to be taught to hide, to live in fear, to be ashamed, and to feel guilt for the people that God created us to be. In accordance, because we now judge what is good or bad, we begin to judge others and ourselves according to the image of perfection that we have conjured up in our minds, and we base our concept of morality by our own reason and logic.

Not that God did not know where Adam was, or that is was possible for Adam. Eve, or anyone, to hide from God, but when God responded, He was not mad because they were naked. Rather, He was mad because they realized that they were naked. In other words, He was mad that they now believed that who He created them to be was to be hid, felt shameful and guilty for, and to be hid. He is still asking man the same question; who told us that who He created wasn't good enough? God did give them skins to cover themselves but this was only to accommodate them in the state they were in. It was never Gods' intent that we were to hide our nakedness. The Law was given as a skin. It did not tell them to hide, but rather the Law merely set limitations on how they could express who they are. After God asked them who told them they were naked, what was their response?

Eve blamed the serpent, and Adam, indirectly, blamed God; he told God that if He didn't give him the woman, then they wouldn't be in that situation. How often do we use the actions of others toward us, to justify our reasons for hiding, feeling shame, guilt, etc.? Many of us even go to the extent of living contrary to our personality in an effort to strengthen and protect ourselves. This too is contrary to Christ. I honestly do not believe that the fruit affected Eve until Adam ate the fruit also. The reason why I believe this is because God created man to be the conduit through which woman can gain access to Him. Prior to the "fall of man" the love that Adam showed toward Eve was perfect and unconditional. There were no strings attached, and he accepted her for who God created her to be. It wouldn't surprise me to learn that Eve was 300 lbs., and would be considered everything but attractive by today's standards. The "pictures" that we have of Eve come from the imaginations of men during the renaissance of Europe, highly unlikely that they gave an accurate depiction of Eve, or Adam for that matter.

We tend to attribute our idea of perfect as being that of Gods' also. Anyway, after they ate the fruit, God set a rule based on the change in condition. God knew that in order for creation to continue, man and woman still had to be intimate. Therefore, He set the man to rule over the woman, but now man had the capacity to love with selfish motive. Even though God knew the change in man, He also knew that man was the woman's only way to Him. Thus, God made it inherent in all women that their desire will be toward their husbands. Still today, women are in search of their perfect husband, which they once had. If God creates a woman with the desire to be married, until she finds that husband, that can lead her back to God, she is literally headless.

Women today prove this in that they grasp at almost anything, hoping that what they have taken hold of, is that which they desire. As Paul writes, Christ is the Head of the man, and man is the head of the woman (See, I Corinthians 11:3). Today, even most Christian women rebel against the natural order of what God has put in place. The main reason for this is that men have the tendency to be selfish in their motives for love. In the past, men have repressed, abused, and disregarded the needs and desires of women. The main reason why this is so today is because men for at least the last 100 years are told that being vulnerable in unmanly. Today another extreme is emerging.

Men, in their effort to be vulnerable, forgot that being a man included being a leader, not a follower. Thus, we have effeminate men running around, for lack of a better term, have no balls. As Christian men, we are suppose to love our Christian women (not just our wives and female family members) as Christ loves the Church, but we are also told to be leaders who are following Christ. (See, Ephesians 5:22-23).

Therefore, we are suppose to unselfishly help our Christian sisters become the women that God created them to be, not who we desire them to be. Also, we must be able to lead them in the ways of God. Especially in this age of "feminism",

Satan is still toying with our women by getting them to look for husbands that appeal to their lusts (specification), and in many instances, men that will not require them to be vulnerable. It is a sad commentary, but most Christian men and women, equate beauty on a skin seep level, and identify their sexuality as being the genitals between their legs. Thus, many choose mates based on shared hobbies, bank account numbers, shared likes, etc., but very few choose mated based on real issues, such as emotional, mental, and sexual compatibility; the greatest sex organ we have is the mind, not genitals.

Today, we see the results of the Tree of Knowledge all around us, in every aspect of life. Children and adults are seeking their identity based on things, and others, outside of themselves. They are attaining to others standards of what will bring them happiness and contentment. Many waste their time and money in an effort to conform to the image which others pronounce as beautiful, acceptable, and worthy. This mind set, throughout history- "there is nothing new under the sun"-, has caused mankind to go through era's of repression and rebellion. In a state of repression, the soul yearns to be who God created it to be, and accomplish the things that it is meant to do.

In the state of rebellion, shame, guilt and fear set in, causes drug use, alcoholism (so to can repression), which eventually causes us to be lost altogether, or sends us back into hiding and repression- us telling God what is good or bad for us, and by what specifications He must meet our desires.

In both states, repression and rebellion, we are serving as our own gods. In repression we believe that we can perfect ourselves, by our own standards- whether this is self-induced or adopted from others. In rebellion, we believe that we are the masters of our own destiny, and nothing can, or better, get in our way. The end result is that neither will give us the satisfaction or peace which we desire, and that God desires to give us. The first step that must be taken is to submit ourselves to the One that created us; that being God. Who better to tell us who He intended us to be than the very One who first imagined us in His perfect mind.

We are created in the likeness of God, but that likeness is the soul, not the body. God is a spirit, not a body. The body is merely a vessel given to us so that His creation can be manifested in this plane of existence. There are also other planes of existence, which we do not perceive with the physical eye. When God came to earth, He took on the likeness of man, not Himself, and He was called Jesus (See, Philippians 2:7-11). The only way to gain access to the Creator is through Jesus Christ, because the Creator manifested Himself as Jesus. Thus it is written that by Him all things were created (See, Colossians 1:15-18).

Therefore, if one is not a Christian, they have no ability to find out who God created them to be. Without Christ, we all have, and sadly many still do, try to make our own ways to God, based on what sounds logical, reasonable, wise and probable according to our own image of whom we believe God is. Thus we create our own gods, and we put these gods before the true and living God.

Almost everyone, if not everyone, has at one time in their life lied to another, disobeyed their parents, and have taken something that didn't belong to them. Therefore, we are all sinners, and are in need of salvation. That salvation is available only through Jesus Christ.

You may not believe that, and that is your choice. Though no matter what we believe or thinks, it does not change Gods' truth. Likewise, no matter what we think, unless by an act of God to save us, if we jump out of a plane with no parachute, our bodies will be shattered on impact with the Earth - the natural law of gravity, which God put in place, dictates that this is so.

Thus, the first vulnerability we must embrace is that we, living by our own standards, are a mess in need of help.

We must humble ourselves, which is vulnerability, and own up to the fact that we are wrong. Only when we do this can we go to our Creator and ask Him who we are, and what His purpose is for us. Once we have accepted the Way in which God provided, He tells us the next steps. We are to seek first the Kingdom of God, and His righteousness (See. Matthew 6:33). Then, and only then, will al the things which will fulfill and compliment us will be added to us.

God knows everything that is needed for us to be the people that He created us to be. Though, where is the Kingdom of God? Jesus tells us that it is not a kingdom which can be observed. Nobody can draw a map and direct us to it.

The journey will be unique, yet in some ways similar, for every individual; not all people need the same things, in the same way. There is no cookie cutter form which all must conform to. Why? The Kingdom of God is within each of us, in the form of Gods' image for us.

All of the images together build the Kingdom of God. Does this mean that Hindus and Buddhists are right? No, because the only way this kingdom can be revealed to us is if the Holy Ghost is there to reveal it.

As Jesus says, we must be born again in order to see and enter the Kingdom (See, Luke 17:20-21, John 3:3). Gods' image, and therefore the Kingdom of God, is also within the unbeliever, but they cannot see, or access, the Kingdom without the King- Christ Jesus. This Kingdom is within us in the form of the soul- that which God created in His likeness.

Inside the soul carried the image of God for each individual; our desires, passions, sexuality, drive, etc.

All of these things are Gods' image for us. This leads us to the second step in the formula that Jesus gave us. That is we must seek Gods' righteousness. Here is where most Christians fly off Gods' radar, and send them on a vain quest of self-perfection. The righteousness of God does not come by the Law- we cannot perfect ourselves, especially when most Christians' image of a perfect Christian is not Gods', but mans. If righteousness does come by the Law, then our belief in Jesus is foolishness, and He died in vain (See, Galatians 2:21).

Today, many Christians try to eradicate, and rid themselves, of the passions, desires, etc. because some "ministers" have twisted the Word of God into a lie. Christ is the end of the Law for righteousness to everyone that believes in Him (See, Romans 10:1-11). There are no buts or ands. What then? We are simply told to love our neighbor as we love ourselves. If we do this, we will not steal from them, murder them, despitefully use them for selfish motives, be jealous of them, hide from them, etc. When we do these things, we judge who is and who isn't worthy, we tell God that He held back on us, etc., and we tell God what is good and bad for us. When Paul perceived a flaw in himself, he did not say to stress over it, to go beat himself, etc. Instead, Jesus told him not to worry about it.

> "My grace is sufficient for thee: for my strength is made perfect in weakness" (II Corinthians 12:7-9)

Christ wants us to be free of the guilt, shame, fear, and insecurity that prevents Him from performing His work in our lives. He wants us to quit eating of the fruit of the Tree of Knowledge, which is carnal wisdom, and start resting and learning of Him. He wants us to again be naked. He wants us to grow and be the people that God created us to be, without apology to anything or anybody else. As Paul says, it should be a very matter to us who are in Christ, that another, even ourselves, judge us (See, I Cor. 4:1-6). Even when our hearts condemn us, we are told to find comfort in the fact that God is greater than our hearts and knows all things.

As we grow in Him, as we learn more of Him and begin to embrace our vulnerabilities, our heart will no longer condemn us because we will know who we are, is of God, and thus we will grow in confidence toward God (See, John 3:18-24). Thus, our vulnerabilities become the strength and power of Christ. Those we will meet will wonder how we have obtained such confidence, and yet we stay humble.

Then we can testify of the power of Christ in us. But if we go about to be strong, and perfect ourselves, we lose the power of Christ, and we subject ourselves to be Satan's' play toy, even though we are Christians. If we try to make ourselves strong, we are relying on ourselves, not Christ. When we allow others, or ourselves, to dictate what is good or bad for us, we conform to mans' image, not Gods' image for us. We all have desires, passions, fantasies, hopes, dreams, etc.

For these things not to be fulfilled in us, because we choose to repress or ignore them, it is rebellion against God. This is why many Christians suffer frustration; they are working against the will of God for their lives. To the Spiritually minded, all things are possible, we will find, we will receive, and the door will be opened to us. Therefore, those who are living in the Spirit are free, and they live in constant expectation of God fulfilling their desires, and adding to their lives those things which will bring contentment, peace, and joy. Also, every experience is seen as an opportunity.

God will give us the desires of our heart, but He will not cater to our specifications; which are lusts. If we desire a car, he will provide but He won't promise a specific make, model, color, etc...If we desire to get married, He will provide, but He will not cater to hair types, body builds, etc. He is only concerned with fulfilling our desires, and He can fulfill our desires beyond our wildest expectations. He will give us that which will fulfill, compliment, and enhance every aspect of our lives. This does not mean that we are to idly sit and wait for things to fall into our laps. If we believe Him, we will go in search of the promise, we must look to find, and knock for the door to be opened.

Then we must be willing to advertise who we are- stand naked before others. As they say, a closed mouth never gets fed. How can anyone know what we are seeking unless we tell them? But we must also be specific. To say I am romantic could mean something totally different to another who thinks himself romantic also.

Therefore, we must discuss the hows and whys about ourselves also. It makes no sense for another person of the same sex to know everything about us intimately, and then expect a member of the opposite sex to read our minds.

When we are free in Christ, and naked, we will repel those who might cause us harm, before there is any potential for them to hurt us. Also, even if another hurts us, rejects us, etc. We will not be shaken from our foundation, or be inclined to sacrifice ourselves just to be accepted. It is one thing to be self-confident, but it is another thing altogether to have confidence in self. Confidence in self type of people want others to know who they are so that a mutual understanding is met before any type of relationship proceeds. Jesus was confident in self, He was bold in who He was, and really didn't care what others thought of Him.

Confident in self people identify themselves with the Master of who they are, and if that Master is Christ, there is no reason to feel guilt, shame, fear, or insecurity. It is my hope that all have been edified, and that some bonds have been broken.

If you would like to respond to this, and potentially learn more, I would love to hear from you.

Please write to: Paul Richard Jr. Curran c/o 92B0374

www.**foundationuniversitypress**.com

ti

www.ingramcontent.com/pod-product-compliance
Lightning Source LLC
Chambersburg PA
CBHW020244130626
46549CB00005B/2048